FASHIONING THE NATION

FASHIONING THE NATION

Costume and Identity in British Cinema

PAM COOK

BFI PUBLISHING

First published in 1996 by the
British Film Institute
21 Stephen Street
London W1P 2LN

The British Film Institute exists to promote appreciation,
enjoyment, protection and development of moving image
culture in and throughout the whole of the United Kingdom.
Its activities include the National Film and Television
Archive; the National Film Theatre; the Museum of the
Moving Image; the London Film Festival; the production
and distribution of film and video; funding and support for
regional activities; Library and Information Services; Stills,
Posters and Designs; Research; Publishing and Education;
and the monthly *Sight and Sound* magazine.

British Library Cataloguing in Publication Data.
A catalogue record for this book is available from the British Library.

ISBN: 0–85170–574–X pbk

Cover still: Jean Kent in *Caravan* (Arthur Crabtree, 1946)
Cover design by MetaUnion

Typeset by Fakenham Photosetting Ltd,
Fakenham, Norfolk
Printed in Great Britain by The Trinity Press,
Worcester

For my mother and father, with love

ACKNOWLEDGMENTS

In the short time at my disposal, I have had to rely heavily on secondary sources, and I am indebted to those indefatigable historians whose original work in the archives has made my speculative, selective survey of ideas about national identity in British cinema possible. I hope I have adequately represented that work. I am particularly grateful to BFI Education and Research for allowing me five months in 1992 out of my job on *Sight and Sound* to think, learn and write.

My editor Duncan Petrie's enthusiasm for British cinema has been a constant source of inspiration, and his generous support for this project, beyond the call of friendship, has been invaluable. I am deeply indebted to Catherine Surowiec, who took time out from working on her definitive study of cinema design to look at the Elizabeth Haffenden filmography and to suggest additions and corrections. The staff of BFI Publishing, in particular Roma Gibson, Dawn King, John Smoker and Sue Bobbermein, demonstrated their usual high level of professionalism, patience and willingness to help with technical and other advice. Thanks, too, to Vicky Grut for her astute copy editing.

Since my research began, a number of people have offered various kinds and degrees of support. Special thanks are due to Ed Buscombe, James Donald, Richard Dyer, Lizzie Francke, Sue Harper, Janet Hawken, Andrew Higson, Nick James, Colin MacCabe, Laura Marcus, Jill McGreal, Andy Medhurst, Janet Moat, Geoffrey Nowell-Smith, Colette O'Reilly, Sylvia Paskin, Esther Ronay, Rebecca Russell, Jackie Stacey, Lisa Tickner, John O. Thompson, Ginette Vincendeau and Tana Wollen. Above all, my love and thanks go to Sam Cook for her gypsy spirit.

CONTENTS

I

INTRODUCTION: MIXING IT

In an article in a leading quality newspaper, Richard Gott bewails the vacuum at the heart of British culture, laying the blame for the lack of a dynamic indigenous literature, theatre, music or cinema on the post-war US invasion, which colonised the hearts and minds of the English to the extent that we now see ourselves as Anglo-Americans (Gott, 1994). The brief love affair with the idea of a progressive, unified Europe that held sway in the 80s, offering the possibility of cultural as well as political alliances, has, argues Gott, disintegrated as 'Europe' has disappeared, leaving us with an adulterated cosmopolitan culture, derived from the USA, in which nothing is authentic. Such residual national culture as remains is in the form of nostalgia for a lost past – the ill-remembered 'heritage' celebrated by Merchant Ivory films and Hovis commercials, of which Gott is suitably, given his brief, contemptuous:

> For the English today, it seems, there is no national culture alter-native, except nostalgia – the construction of a largely bogus heritage. This is where the residual cultural nationalism of England has taken refuge these last few years, in pursuit of an ill-remembered past – where the decades and the centuries are hopelessly intermingled. Historical novels, Merchant Ivory films, Victorian lamp standards all form part of this bizarre phenomenon. And is there Hovis still for tea? Understandably perhaps, faced with a choice between 'Anglo-America' and 'English Heritage', a substantial majority of the population still clearly favours the former (Gott, 1994, p. 29).

Disguised as polemic, Gott's article trots out a number of well-worn themes. His argument is suffused with longing for a genuinely English culture, uncontaminated by foreign influences – particularly the degraded popular culture of the USA. This is, perhaps, not such an extraordinary position in an age of global communications; but it is

1

certainly to misrecognise the nature of culture itself, which is always a mixture of national and international, specific and general, interior and exterior. Even the indigenous Irish and Scottish art celebrated by Gott cannot be entirely pure – if it were, no one else would understand it. This is equally true of national cinemas; to be recognised as such, and to survive, they must speak to an international audience, and their cultural differences be readable by outsiders.

Even more familiar is Gott's despairing sense that English culture is doomed to be caught forever between the colonising onslaught of American cultural imperialism and the maelstrom of Europe, where national boundaries and value systems shift so rapidly and violently that the very notion of 'culture' is called into question. This sense of alienation, ambivalence and loss pervades much writing on national identity. Many commentators reject what they see as the phoney certainties of official versions in favour of more authentic models. Yet, as I argue in the following pages, the quest for authentic identities is itself doomed. Not only does it depend on a process of expulsion of perceived negative, inauthentic elements which inevitably return to haunt the legitimated culture, but identity formation is a fluctuating, fractured affair which militates against any final settlement.

Until very recently, discussion of national identity has failed to take on board the fissures at the heart of identity itself. Yet the world-wide resurgence of ethnocentric nationalisms makes the investigation of the symptomatic status of this phenomenon a priority. Nationalisms which depend on a retreat to cultural purity, to unchanging ethnic identities and boundaries, appear to be a manifestation of cultural crisis, a last refuge from social change. The search for purity is self-evidently untenable, since the expelled pollutants come from within, which is where they really belong and where they always return. Thus identity is, from the beginning, lacerated, torn between self and other.

If nationalism can be seen as an attempt to heal the wound at the heart of national identity, it also appeals to a fundamental desire to find a 'home', an imagined place where unified, stable identities nurtured by common interests can flourish. This conception, inevitably shaded by infantile longing, often relies on traditional gender roles of patriarchal authority overseeing maternal sacrifice. Yet it is never, of course, that simple. The heroic, patriotic version of national identity frequently conflicts with the intimate, domestic variety, rupturing the home culture and its sustaining fantasy of community, which is often conflated with family. During the First World War, for example, many women left behind in England identified strongly with their brothers and fathers fighting overseas and were deeply frustrated by their home-front role (see Light, 1991). And, indeed, internal ethnic divisions always threaten to unpick the fraying seams of national unity. 'Home', in the sense of a tranquil, safe place, becomes an ever-receding object, swiftly turning into its opposite, the locus of uncertainty and anomie. Freud's notion of the uncanny, the twinning of the *heimlich* and *unheimlich*, is revelatory here, for the safety of home (*heim*) is inseparable from its strangeness (Freud, 1990). The place to which we belong is also foreign to us.

What becomes clear in my survey of discourses of national identity in Chapter II is that the role of women in formations of national culture is by no means straightforward. Those official versions in the 30s and 40s that stress a home-centred femininity perceived in terms of self-sacrifice and submission to goals of national unity and stability must be seen in the context of the general cultural reassessment of notions of femininity between the wars. What Alison Light has described as the domestication of British culture during this period saw the rise of conflicting definitions of what it meant to be female. As significant as the suburbanised 'little England' ethos of stoical 'ordinary' people muddling through, was the restless desire to escape the confines of 'home' in search of adventure and exoticism abroad. While for male writers, this often resulted in the rejection of a feminised homeland in favour of exile, for women it meant the search for new identities of class, gender and nation – as in Daphne Du Maurier's historical fiction, for example (Light, 1991).

'Escapist' literature of this sort, populated by gypsies, pirates and smugglers and featuring heroes and heroines dedicated to wandering over land and sea, was prevalent during the 30s and resurfaced in the 40s with the wartime intensification of social mobility. This vagrant spirit provided the inspiration for the Gainsborough costume romances considered in Chapter V. These films were often adaptations of popular middlebrow novels: clearly, the anti-consensual themes of such escapist fare held a powerful appeal for women readers and cinemagoers. Yet the implications for cultural formations of nation and gender of this romance with other times and places have rarely been taken on board, even in revisionist discussions of national identity (for example, Hurd, 1984; Lant, 1991; Higson, 1995).

Despite the fact that the search for unified identities is demonstrably flawed, the need for authentic versions of national identities strongly persists, even in sophisticated theoretical accounts. The critical destabilisation of national identity may have shifted the bases towards more complex, fluid definitions of identity formation. But it has not yet entirely dislodged the wish for the apparent certainties offered by an 'authentic' national culture, however that may be formulated. It is not my intention here to dissolve national identity altogether, nor to deny the significance of nationalist political and cultural struggle. My project is rather to explore the possibility of changing places, in both senses of the phrase, offered by the process of splitting that is characteristic of identity formation, in which the self is a labile amalgam of other identities rather than a fixed entity. My primary metaphor is one of travel, through and between different identities in a constant movement of exile and return which must transform the notion of homeland. As travellers, we cross boundaries and, through identification with other cultures, acquire a sense of ourselves as something more than national subjects. This may smack of cultural tourism – but what is culture, after all, if not a collection of souvenirs?

This notion of exile and return has implications for the business of cinema-going. Although, following Mulvey (1989a), film theory has tended to stress the reinforcement of (male) ego, it has been suggested more recently (for example, by Donald, 1992) that the operations of fantasy in cinema require an approach that recognises the dependency of fantasy on transgressive desire. This implies that loss of the boundaries of identity is at least as important to pleasure in cinema as the shoring up of ego. Indeed, it has been argued that in certain genres, such as melodrama, horror or comedy, the final return to the status quo is precarious, to say the least. The loss of self involved in identification with characters or immersion in narrative processes can be seen as a kind of travelling in which the wanderer can return 'home' with a different perspective. This idea of the transforming potential of the cinematic experience, playing on the fluidity of identity, opens the way to an adventure in which identities are tried and tested rather than simply bolstered.

When it comes to national identity in cinema, this vagrancy metaphor comes into its own. It opens the way to border crossings which potentially enable us to imagine ourselves world citizens rather than, or as well as, national subjects. Indeed, I would argue that many of us do, in practice, think of ourselves in terms of multiple identities. The demand for a culturally specific, indigenous British cinema, in so far as it depends on a notion that there is a bedrock, coherent Britishness available to be called up, closes down on this process, though it can never entirely do so. Even the quintessentially English Ealing comedies – *Passport to Pimlico*

4

(Henry Cornelius, 1949), for example – are impelled to test national boundaries; while the film that heralded the 80s British challenge to Hollywood, *Chariots of Fire* (Hugh Hudson, 1981), is precisely about the problem of Britishness. Nevertheless, despite critical attempts to rehabilitate the internationalist impulse of the likes of Powell and Pressburger and the Gainsborough melodramas (Christie, 1985; Aspinall and Murphy, 1983; Barr, 1986), it is the cosy, parochial Englishness typified by Ealing, and its attendant realist aesthetic, that have continued to stand for 'British cinema', perpetuating a consensus view of that cinema as dominated by restraint and repression. No other British studio or body of films has been accorded this status – which seems extraordinary when one considers the varieties of Englishness on offer in Hammer horror, say, or the *Carry On* burlesques, or Alexander Korda historical epics.

The continuing success of Ealing in representing British cinema in the popular imagination resides in its air of authenticity – achieved by using realism to (finally) confirm a coherent, unified national identity. Ealing movies lack the element of pastiche common to Hammer, *Carry On* comedies and the Korda spectaculars, and it is pastiche that is the undoing of authentic identities. Pastiche suggests hybridity rather than purity, which helps to explain why realism is often the preferred aesthetic in official prescriptions for national cinema. Pastiche smacks of fraud – it questions the very idea of originality or essence. The construction of British cinema in terms of authenticity and realism has had significant effects on the writing of its history and on debates around its national identity. These have tended to concentrate on the 40s struggles to establish a consensus on how our national cinema should be constituted, and have sustained the consensus by focusing on officially sanctioned, realist 'quality' films, even when questioning the limits of consensus. In critical discourse reassessing British cinema, anti-consensual films, such as those of Powell and Pressburger and Gainsborough, have come to be seen as a kind of underground current going against the tide of British cinema 'proper' – a position which almost wilfully ignores their popularity (in box-office terms, at least) at the time of their release (see Lant, 1991, pp. 231–3). In fact, the wartime realist quality films were relatively few in number and were not always that successful in the domestic market. Yet they have attracted an inordinate amount of critical attention.

My own focus on a handful of 40s costume romances may seem equally restricted. It is motivated by the fact that the anti-consensual themes of these films have consistently been marginalised, ignored or subsumed into the consensus in discussion of British cinema (see, for example, Hurd, 1984; Richards, 1988; Lant, 1991; Higson, 1995). It is my contention that films that do not subscribe to officially sanctioned strictures on the construction of a quality national cinema are not marginal aberrations, but are central to any reassessment of British cinema. It seems to me essential to widen the parochial terms in which discussion has been couched so far.

Gainsborough is crucial in this respect, because as a studio it set out from the beginning to be more than British, looking outwards towards Hollywood and Europe for both an identity and an aesthetic. Gainsborough's involvement in the Film Europe movement of the late 20s and 30s, when founder Michael Balcon actively sought out co-production deals with Germany and imported foreign technicians, gave the studio and its output a distinctly international character (Higson, 1993b). It seems ironic that Balcon went on to set up Ealing on almost directly opposed principles, leaving behind the 'expressionism' that he had previously prized so highly as a guarantee of quality. Gainsborough's international leanings have almost certainly contributed to the studio's ambiguous status in British cinema, particularly during the Second World War, when it was heresy to suggest that national identity might be mixed.

Yet this is precisely what the wartime Gainsborough costume dramas under consideration do suggest – indeed, they go further, putting identity itself in crisis through narratives of schizophrenia and amnesia and cross-cultural love affairs. British audiences at the time were invited to identify with British stars playing French, Spanish, Italian and ethnically mixed characters, and to journey into a fictionalised 'Europe' which called into question many of the prevailing notions of Britishness. Some of these films included a 'who am I, where am I?' scenario in which characters caught in identity crisis and memory loss provided a mirror for audience members experiencing an analogous loss of identity in the darkness of the cinema.

It is no coincidence that it was costume drama in which such adventures in hybridity took place. Costume drama, with its emphasis on masquerade, is a prime vehicle for exploration of identity, encouraging cross-dressing not only between characters, but metaphorically between characters and spectators, in the sense that the latter can be seen as trying on a variety of roles in the course of the film. Costume drama is also notoriously inauthentic, as any costume historian will testify (Hollander, 1974; Maeder, 1987). Despite extensive and meticulous period

6

research, anachronisms and geographical transgressions abound – indeed, they are endemic to the genre. This element of travesty is closely related to pastiche in its mixing of styles, and it militates against fixed identities in a similar way. It is significant that travesty, masquerade and pastiche are central features of those recent costume films which consciously attempt to recast national and sexual identities, such as Julie Dash's *Daughters of the Dust* (1991), Derek Jarman's *Edward II* (1991), Sally Potter's *Orlando* (1993) or Jane Campion's *The Piano* (1993). The pastiche factor may also have something to do with the contempt in which recent 'heritage' films are held by critics on the Left, who are fond of dismissing them as phoney, contaminated versions of history which mask the 'true' account of our national past (for example, Higson, 1993a).

Despite the fact that costume films are a staple of most national cinemas, they remain virgin territory critically (see, however, Harper, 1994). My symptomatic analysis attempts to explain why this should be so, as well as to stimulate further research. The recent resurgence of costume drama, and the genre's apparent success with female audiences, suggest that it is ripe for further investigation. It appears that costume drama's perceived 'femininity', conflated with inauthenticity, may be responsible to some extent for the critical opprobrium in which it is widely held. Certainly, the pivot of my argument about the Gainsborough costume romances is their particular conjunction of femininity, foreignness and masquerade, which put them beyond the pale of wartime quality British cinema. These flamboyant films reinscribed the feminine principle, defined in terms of a transgressive, itinerant spirit, in history. By implication, the reassessment of femininity is central to any discussion about national identity in and of 'British' cinema.

In the pages that follow, the repression of the feminine is a recurring theme. The word 'repression' is often used in relation to British cinema, particularly when it comes to sexuality (see, for example, Ellis, 1975; Hurd, 1984; Dyer, 1994). Yet the notion of repression is a little misleading, suggesting as it does that there is an authentic femininity available to be reinstated at will. It seems more feasible to think in terms of competing definitions of femininity to which different value is attached at specific historical moments. At any particular time, there are multiple social definitions, sanctioned and unsanctioned, offering a variety of possible identifications for individuals and groups to try out. Those definitions that are unsanctioned – that is, relegated or devalued – are none the less available for identification. Indeed, despite official attempts

7

to control such fluidity, they may, by virtue of being transgressive, exert a more powerful appeal than those that are sanctioned.

Antonia Lant (1991) has identified at least two official versions of femininity in play during the Second World War: an overtly sexual, eroticised female image projected as highly dangerous to national security, and the deglamorised 'mobile women', decked out in utility gear, who stood in for absent men (no doubt there were other definitions too: the maternal, nurturing woman, for example). While official discourses attempted to manage the gender slippage attendant on social mobility, there is reason to suppose that many women took advantage of the opportunity to cross-dress in masculine drag – the dungarees, uniforms and tailored suits sanctioned by official sumptuary regulations. But in the context of wartime restrictions on clothing and cosmetics, the sexualised, glamorous woman was an equally powerful image. The role of popular fictions, cinematic and otherwise, can be seen to rehearse shifts between multiple identifications, in some cases settling in favour of stability, in others, keeping the play of identities open. But even those that strive for settlement cannot hope to police the responses of audiences.

My enquiry points the way to many other areas which demand attention, among them, the historical relationship of British cinema to Europe, for too long eclipsed by the preoccupation with Hollywood 'domination'. Gainsborough's adoption of European-influenced aesthetics, discussed in Chapter V, is relevant here – indeed, the impact of European art movements on British cinema has scarcely begun to be addressed. The idea that our national cinema might consist of a heterogeneous amalgam of visual styles and formal strategies appropriated from other cultures appears to be anathema to those concerned with constructing its identity. Yet such heterogeneity is what all cultures are made of. The British often appear to be as ambivalent towards Europe as they are towards the USA. Nevertheless, as Ian Christie has pointed out in relation to Powell and Pressburger, the internationalist leaning towards assimilation of other cultures runs deep in British society (Christie, 1985). And, following this line of investigation, far too little is known about the effects of demographic changes in 30s and 40s Britain on both cinema audiences and studio personnel. In the absence of hard statistical information, misleading assumptions are sometimes made about the ethnic, class and gender constitution of British audiences.

The contribution of costume designers and art directors has been scandalously neglected, reflecting the lack of discussion of visual aesthetics in British cinema. Costume design in particular is a sphere in which women have made their mark. In Chapter III, I consider some of the reasons for its neglect. The association of screen costume with fashion has not helped its case. Not only is costume generally perceived as deeply embedded in the Hollywood system of commodity production through fashion tie-ins, but it is seen by some theorists as commodifying the viewing process itself, encouraging a fetishistic relationship between audience and image. Recent work on costume as a signifying system in its own right (for example, Gaines, 1990) has reassessed notions of fetishism and masquerade to open up a more complex view of the contribution of screen dress to the process of making meaning – not just in relation to the films themselves, but to the activities and discourses surrounding them. Rather than simply being the dupes of the cinematic experience, spectators have come to be seen as active participants, using both images and commodities in their own interests.

There is also the question of studio style, commonplace in studies of Hollywood, but almost absent from discussion of British cinema. Gainsborough provides a particularly interesting case study in this respect. Unlike Ealing, say, or Hammer, for which it has been possible to construct core identities, Gainsborough's frequent changes of personnel have made it difficult to identify a consistent studio style – either of management or aesthetics. Paradoxically, this can be seen as a strength. Gainsborough successfully negotiated the ups and downs of the British film industry during the 20s and 30s, becoming a key player in industry policy during that time. The shifts in style manifested in its output are symptomatic of historical changes in British film culture during a crucial period of its development. These are just some of the avenues open to exploration.

This book can be used in several ways. Each chapter is intended to stand alone as a discussion of a particular topic or area. Nevertheless, there are themes that range across chapters, and my argument is developed in such a manner as to suggest a journey through debates and issues that has no final destination – nor, indeed, a prescribed starting point. Whatever route the reader takes, I hope the journey is a pleasurable one.

II

BREAKING THE CONSENSUS ON BRITISH CINEMA

In 1940, the Ministry of Information Films Division issued official guidelines to British studios outlining the ways in which the film industry should contribute to the war effort by devoting itself to producing effective propaganda. This 'Programme for Film Propaganda' (reprinted in Christie, 1978) outlined the terms for representing the British at war not only to all-important home-front audiences, but to the rest of the world (that is, the Continent, the USA and the Dominions). The directive defined the British way of life and character, national ideals and institutions schematically, to say the least: independence, toughness of fibre, sympathy with the underdog, love of freedom and democracy, and a capacity for sacrifice. The memorandum also offered aesthetic advice, including suggestions for suitable themes and narrative resolutions, and for ways of dramatising contemporary events to disguise the propaganda element. A *caveat* recognised cultural differences:

> Pictures of English liberty and honour welcomed at home are interpreted on the Continent as evidence of slackness and stupidity. Shots of our soldiers laughing or playing football must be cut out of all newsreels and documentaries sent to France. So sharp is the division that it will be necessary to make documentary films specially for France and neutral countries (Christie, 1978, p.123).

In effect, this was also a 'Programme for a National Cinema', a contribution to current debates about how a successful indigenous cinema was to be constituted. Such arguments, representing the conflicting vested interests of film-makers, critics, audiences and official bodies, though given added urgency by the Second World War, have never been far from the surface. Indeed, it is in the nature of national cinemas, or cultures, to be obsessed with their identity. The British compulsion to fix the parameters of its native cinema goes back as far as its inception, and is bound up with more general cultural developments. There is a fascinating history to be written, unfortunately beyond the scope of this book, about this interrelationship. Here, I focus on a particular period (the 40s) that has been perceived as a golden moment in British cinema history, in that homegrown product projecting specifically national concerns achieved unusual box-office success in a domestic market 'dominated' by Hollywood (Lant, 1991, pp. 231–3).

Post-war British historians return again and again to this period. It is an incredibly fertile area for study, not only because of its landmark films, but because of structural changes in the industry, which allowed for a flowering of independent production and gave rise to a lively diversity of output (Ellis, 1978). This diversity has scarcely been recognised, even by those 70s pioneers who set out to rescue British cinema from the dustbin of mediocrity to which it had been consigned in the 50s and 60s, when the auteur theory captivated all self-respecting cinephiles. By and large, discussion of national identity in 40s British cinema has focused on the consensus films – that is, those on which an uneasy alliance of opinion between producers and critics (mainly from the quality press) and official bodies such as the Ministry of Information Films Division, the Foreign Office and the British Board of Film Censors conferred the status of quality British cinema. Generally, these were films set in contemporary British locales, addressing specifically national issues and adopting an aesthetic of restrained realism.

Audiences, however, often failed to agree with the consensus. The critically sanctioned films were not always successful at the box office (Lant, 1991, pp. 231–3). In fact, a relatively small number of films achieved quality status. Some titles might be: *In Which We Serve* (David Lean and Noel Coward, 1942), *Millions Like Us* (Frank Launder and Sidney Gilliat, 1943), *This Happy Breed* (David Lean, 1944), *The Way Ahead* (Carol Reed, 1944) and *Waterloo Road* (Sidney Gilliat, 1944) (Lant, 1991, pp. 41–56). Both *Millions Like Us* and *Waterloo Road* were produced by Gainsborough Studios, the subject of my final chapter. The wartime consensus has been perpetuated by the narrow focus adopted by subsequent commentators. Little wonder, then, that British cinema has so often been written off as universally parochial, with brief flashes of brilliance from the likes of Powell and Pressburger and David Lean.

However, this is not a plea for greater recognition of British cinema's wonderful diversity, important though that is. There are in any case

11

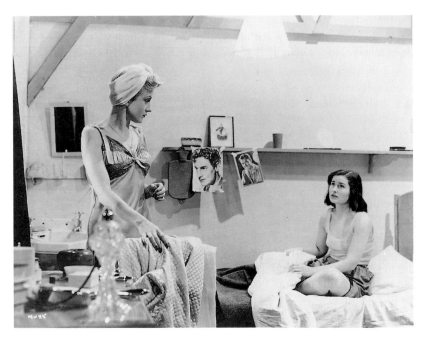

Undressing national subjects: *Millions Like Us*

recent signs that the consensus is tearing at the seams (Barr, 1986; Murphy, 1989; Landy, 1991). The low-rent status of our national cinema in comparison with others has often been put down to a critical failure: an innate sense of cultural inferiority permeates much post-war writing on the subject (see Barr, 1986). It is interesting that the famous essay on Englishness in English art by German expatriate Nikolaus Pevsner levels precisely the same accusation at British critics such as Roger Fry who write disparagingly about their own artistic traditions (Pevsner, 1956). The answer obviously is, as Charles Barr and others argue in *All Our Yesterdays* (Barr, 1986), to change the terms of critical discussion and the way in which British cinema has been perceived. However, I want to take a slightly different tack.

In his introduction to *All Our Yesterdays*, Barr, taking a cue from Harold Wilson – President of the Board of Trade in the late 40s and with a more than passing interest in film – characterises approaches to British cinema, and, indeed, that cinema itself, in terms of amnesia and schizophrenia, positing his book as part of the process of 'remembering'. It is no coincidence that Barr uses the language of psychological disturbance and identity crisis. Almost everywhere one looks in critical writing about British cinema one finds a fixation on its 'Britishness' combined with a deep ambivalence about Britishness itself. This crisis at the heart of our film culture leads me to suspect that the desire for a British cinema with clearly defined national boundaries is probably impossible and in any case undesirable. I shall argue that attempts to establish a core identity for that cinema are similarly flawed. This route will lead me through some of the key writings on the subject over the last twenty years or so in search of signs of stress. At the end of the journey I shall confront the concept of 'national identity' itself.

As already indicated, it is difficult to find writing on British cinema that does not address its Britishness at some level. (There is something rather defensive in this, but as we shall see, defence is a primary mechanism in traditional constructions of national identity.) Certain texts are considered landmarks – Raymond Durgnat's *A Mirror for England* and Charles Barr's *Ealing Studios* among them (Durgnat, 1970; Barr, 1977). Durgnat had been a lone voice among British auteur critics in the mid-60s when he championed the work of Michael Powell in the

Staging everyday life: *Millions Like Us*

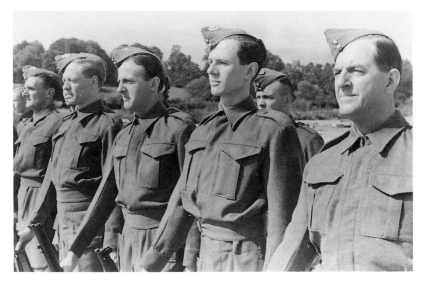

Ironing out difference: *The Way Ahead*

pages of *Movie* magazine, which had generally condemned its native cinema as inferior to Hollywood. In his book he began to map the uncharted territory of British cinema, looking at a range of post-war films for the ways in which they expressed aspects of British society. The 'reflection' motif of his title is apt, since he sees national characteristics, attitudes and social history as directly readable, with very little distortion, from the surface of the movies.

It is easy, with theoretical hindsight, to dismiss Durgnat's approach as simplistic. His polemical defence of a cinema of dissent against what he calls 'the self-satisfied films' (that is, those which affirm national unity) is nevertheless intriguing, as is his idiosyncratic style of writing. Durgnat's technique asserts individuality against consensus, of which he is deeply suspicious. Significant, too, is the detached, ironic tone with which he distances himself from notions of patriotism. The impression is of someone profoundly at odds with his own culture. Yet Durgnat's individualism and detachment are themselves qualities which are frequently identified as quintessentially English. His book expresses an anxiety at the core of national identity: that individual identity will be swallowed up by it.

The ambivalence in Durgnat's account of British cinema recurs in later studies, as does his notion that 'the English way of life' is a conservative, upper-middle-class construct designed to ward off social discontent. His perception of national character as a coherent, self-contained entity available to be directly expressed through cultural artefacts such as movies also survives, though with some refinements. Charles Barr in *Ealing Studios*, while taking issue with the idea that films can be seen as offering documentary evidence of English life, asserts that they do offer evidence of their makers' vision of that life – in the case of Ealing, a remarkably consistent vision spanning the twenty years of Michael Balcon's leadership. Barr is less ambivalent about consensus than Durgnat, and less phobic about the national values that Ealing represented: the tight-knit, self-sufficient community, thriving on a system of benevolent paternalism, living and working in a suburban idyll surrounded by a neat English garden. For Barr, Ealing judged its audiences' mood well, projecting a fantasy of Britain which captured the nation's imagination, and he celebrates that success. At the same time, he recognises its historical specificity: by the mid-50s the consensus, and Ealing, were played out.

Bringing it all home: Stewart Granger in *Waterloo Road*

Barr is unusual in allowing a productive, creative role to the consensus view of national identity. His book was extremely influential, so much so that Ealing came to stand for British cinema itself. Other writers have been more critical of the studio's cosy parochialism, of the elitism of its working practices and the repressiveness of its espousal of realism (Ellis, 1975). But Barr's book established a core identity for British cinema through a study of one studio's output – something that David Pirie's work on Hammer had not achieved (Pirie, 1973). Many of the themes and formal strategies identified by Barr as characteristic of Ealing's vision of Britain turn up later in more general studies of national identity in British cinema, thus reinforcing the critical consensus about this identity. And this despite the fact that in the mid-80s new work on British cinema – on Powell and Pressburger and Gainsborough Studios in particular (Aspinall and Murphy, 1983; Christie, 1985) – opened up the whole area for discussion.

Durgnat, writing in 1970, had already pointed to aberrant, critical British films, including Powell and Gainsborough among them. In 1978, Ian Christie's *Powell, Pressburger and Others* demonstrated how uneasily their films related to the wartime and post-war consensus on quality British cinema (Christie, 1978). Seven years later in *Arrows of Desire*, Christie elaborated his thesis, emphasising the alien sensibility of Powell and Pressburger's movies and putting this down to a spirit of inter-national collaboration which, though against the English grain, is deeply desired in British culture (Christie, 1985). *Arrows of Desire*, arguing for the anti-consensual impulse of Powell and Pressburger, itself breaks the critical consensus on British cinema, demanding that the contours of debate be adjusted to take account of different cultural and aesthetic traditions.

Christie locates Powell and Pressburger in an anti-realist, formalist, risk-taking tradition, and he sees Derek Jarman, Julien Temple and Neil Jordan as inheriting this mantle (we might also add Sally Potter's name). An important part of his polemic rests on the influence of European émigrés – the Anglophile Hungarians Alexander Korda and Pressburger himself, French cinematographer Georges Périnal, German art directors Alfred Junge and Hein Heckroth, and Austrian actor Anton Walbrook – on Powell and Pressburger's films. Christie might also have included German cameraman Erwin Hillier and Polish composer Allan Gray. One of the striking aspects of much writing on British cinema is its insularity. It clings to a particularly narrow view of Britishness which is defensive, designed to fend off, manage or control invasion from outsiders.

Christie's insistence on the creative input of 'foreigners' is significant, both in illuminating the cultural scandal caused by Powell and Pressburger and in suggesting a different way forward for British cinema history. His remains, however, an isolated voice. The only other major work to take this question seriously is Karol Kulik's biography of Alexander Korda (Kulik, 1975). It is perhaps significant that neither Christie nor Kulik was born in England.

Before *Arrows of Desire* the consensus had already been tested by the appearance in 1983 of a deceptively slim British Film Institute monograph on the flamboyant melodramas produced in the 40s by the little-known but extremely successful British studio, Gainsborough (Aspinall and Murphy, 1983). Like Powell and Pressburger's movies, Gainsborough's wartime melodramas, though successful at the box office (Lant, 1991, pp. 231–3), hit a cultural nerve, provoking extreme hostility from the British quality critics, who were dedicated to notions of a social realist British cinema. Unlike Powell and Pressburger, however, whose films could on one level be defended as art – and they have been defended in these terms since – Gainsborough's pictures during this period drew on popular literary traditions – romantic, middlebrow historical novels which were already best-sellers among women readers.

Gainsborough translated these novels' purple prose into an extravagant and excessive visual language which went against the grain of British restrained realism, evoking decorative and baroque traditions of which British culture has generally been suspicious (see Pevsner, 1956). I want to focus on two aspects of the Gainsborough melodramas to which the BFI monograph drew attention. First, their success with wartime and immediately post-war audiences was in sharp contrast to the reaction they incited from predominantly middle-class critics. This suggests a class bias in the consensus idea of British cinema. Indeed, though reliable box-office information is difficult to come by (see Lant, 1991, pp. 231–3), it appears that several of the critically sanctioned realist films were not that popular – a fact which is rarely taken on board in discussion of them. Second, the Gainsborough melodramas' flagrant display of female sexuality, coded through costume and art direction to produce an eroticised 'feminine' look, was offensive to those same critics, which suggests a gender bias.

In *Arrows of Desire*, Christie complains that in spite of the formidable case for taking Powell and Pressburger seriously, they remain outsiders to the mainstream of academic analysis. He puts this down to the predominantly industrial and ideological perspective of current film studies, but the evidence is that the resistance has much deeper cultural roots. The refusal to take on board the implications of the anti-consensual films of Gainsborough and of Powell and Pressburger is so marked that it begins to appear symptomatic. One example of such symptomatic discourse is provided by Jeffrey Richards in his article on national identity in British wartime cinema for a 1988 anthology (Richards, 1988). Richards argues, paraphrasing Antonio Gramsci, that cinema is one of the structures that transmits and promotes the dominant national ideology and creates and preserves for it a consensus of support:

> There can be alternative views of the national character, but there will always be a dominant one, and it will be the dominant one which will be enshrined in, transmitted by and promoted through popular culture, and in particular by the cinema (Richards, 1988, p. 43).

He goes on to assert that in wartime films, national identity derived almost entirely from English culture, with 'England' being used inter-changeably with 'Britain' to describe the nation, and that he intends to do the same, 'with apologies to the Celtic fringe' (Richards, 1988, p. 44). With no apologies to Jeffrey Richards, it seems to me that there could be no clearer statement of his own desire to promote the dominant national ideology by providing it with consensual support. This becomes even clearer as he traces the themes of this national identity (nostalgia for a pre-Industrial Revolution English countryside, wish for continuity and stability rather than change, espousal of traditional values of duty and service, and of qualities of stoicism, tolerance, humour and individualism) through a handful of films. Even the weird and wonderful *A Canterbury Tale* (Powell and Pressburger, 1944) is made to fit the consensus, and in his penultimate paragraph the Gainsborough melodramas are also put in their place as consensus movies. The viability or otherwise of Richards's readings of the films is not the issue. What seems to me remarkable is the impulse to collapse all differences – of class, ethnicity, region and sexuality – into an overarching, single concept of national identity, which is exactly what the consensus films attempted to do.

Richards's article is a classic case of the cultural amnesia described by Barr in *All Our Yesterdays* (Barr, 1986). Richards appears oblivious to the mid-80s debates about national identity and consensus, or to the dangers of basing judgments on the evidence of a narrow range of movies. Any argument that questions his approach – such as Sue Harper's contention

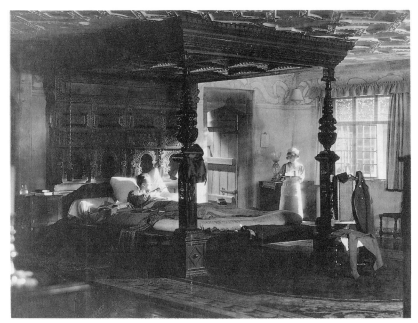

Not exactly English: Alfred Junge's set design for *A Canterbury Tale*

that the Gainsborough melodramas broke the national identity consensus – is swiftly detonated and subsumed (Richards, 1988, p. 59). In trawling British film criticism, one sometimes gets the impression that historians are reluctant to engage with other writers' ideas, or even to recognise them: a further indication of insularity, and of a tendency to fetishise original sources at the expense of intellectual debate.

One of the publications Richards preferred not to recognise was the 1984 collection of essays *National Fictions*, which directly addressed questions of national identity and Second World War cinema (Hurd, 1984). In doing so, the contributors were forced to negotiate a number of methodological problems. One that emerges in several of the articles is the traditional left distrust of nationalism. In 'National Identities', Colin McArthur traces the process of the British Left's reconciliation with nationalism through key texts by Tom Nairn, Ernesto Laclau, Gramsci and Benedict Anderson which suggest that national identity is not the exclusive prerogative of the Right, but can be mobilised in the interests of the Left (McArthur, 1984). Gramsci's concept of hegemony is enlisted by several of the authors to explain the ways in which consensus is formed, through a series of struggles for leadership on the terrain of ideas, values and beliefs. The prevailing idea of national identity at any given historical moment achieves ascendancy only through conflict, through being contested, opposed and resisted, until a compromise equilibrium is formed between competing classes. Thus the Churchillian discourse of national unity based on a heroic imperial past achieved consent during the Second World War (and since then) by virtue of overcoming certain others – such as those which attempted to mobilise popular support on an anti-fascist, anti-imperialist rather than patriotic platform – in spite of a significant political swing to the left in the country during the war. The discourses of resistance were not so much silenced as relegated.

In these terms, the notion of national identity sheds the stigma of right-wing conspiracy to impose a monolithic ideology. Instead, it can be seen as a process of negotiation and transaction in which all classes and groups participate. In spite of this 'cleansing' of nationalism, however, the attitudes of many of the contributors to *National Fictions* remain ambivalent. In 'Our Finest Hour?', Graham Dawson and Bob West argue that in Britain, ideas of patriotism and the nation must be radically transformed before the Left can capture them (Dawson and West, 1984). The former is imbued with nineteenth-century imperialist ideology, while the latter is based on an Anglocentric version of England/Britain which effaces regional and ethnic difference. Dawson and West's critique of British national identity ends with the historical failure of the Left to transform traditional patriotism, and with the assertion that 'the British nation' is now a paranoid fantasy, a symptom of a country's inability to come to terms with its decline.

Writing about the wartime British film industry in 'British Film Production 1939–45', Robert Murphy is less pessimistic, arguing that many of the movies which supported the national consensus made it plain that the sacrifice of class and gender interests to the war effort was to be rewarded by the building of a fairer, more equal post-war society. In one of the few articles to offer a survey of all wartime production, he sounds a *caveat*:

Those films which did express a consensus view of society were only a minority of the films produced by an industry which remained geared to the production of melodramas, mysteries, comedies and musicals (Murphy, 1984, p. 16).

Despite this warning, the case studies comprising the second half of the volume concentrate almost exclusively on consensus movies. In 'Addressing the Nation', Andrew Higson bases his account of the development of a wartime national cinema on the evidence of five officially sanctioned films whose titles recur across the collection (Higson, 1984). On one level, this is a mark of the anthology's origins in a British Film Institute Education Department Summer School which included screenings of these particular films. But this is not really sufficient explanation for the exclusion of anti-consensual material. As a collection, *National Fictions* exhibits signs of schizophrenia: it is split between a desire to break open the national identity consensus and a wish to confirm it. That this should recur in a volume dedicated to a critique of consensus suggests just how strong that consensus is.

Higson's article is valuable in laying out in detail how wartime ideas of national identity translated into the search for a particular kind of national cinema. He stresses the influence of the 30s documentary movement, asserting its key role in the consolidation of British film culture. The films he examines all draw on a rhetoric of realism in which the personal experiences of 'ordinary' people are set in the context of real public events. They are governed by aesthetic restraint, employ a specific iconography and episodic narratives in the effort to define themselves as part of a national cinema clearly distinct from Hollywood. They enjoyed official support, not only from the Ministry of Information, but from contemporary critics concerned with establishing a serious, quality national cinema. Higson identifies formal tensions in the films, particularly around questions of female desire and sexuality. This idea turns up in other articles in the collection and is explored more fully in Antonia Lant's feminist study of national identity in wartime British cinema (Lant, 1991).

But what is striking in Higson's and other contributors' analyses of these realist home-front movies is the absence of the epic, imperialist discourse diagnosed by Dawson and West as central to Churchillian rhetoric. The *Boys' Own* adventure fantasy of masculine heroic exploits conducted on behalf of wives and mothers left weeping at home was significantly shifted in the attempt to come to terms with the real home front experiences of women. The domesticated, feminised version of national identity, which Alison Light in *Forever England* (Light, 1991) describes as emerging after the First World War, holds sway in these movies. However, Higson makes little attempt to explore how and if they contravene official propaganda requirements or prevailing ideas of national identity. Instead, like most of the other contributors, he concentrates on the contradictions and inconsistencies inherent in the project of addressing the nation, evident in the films' textual strategies.

David Lusted's article on *Builders* (Pat Jackson, 1942) and *The Demi-Paradise* (Anthony Asquith, 1943) takes the same tack, demonstrating through detailed analysis how both movies dispute any simple idea of univocal address in wartime propaganda (Lusted, 1984). Lusted also offers some clues as to how the discourse of national identity works, positing an 'us' and 'them' dichotomy. In wartime, 'we' are portrayed positively while 'they', the enemy, are the bearers of negative values. A problem arises when 'they' are our allies rather than the enemy, but allies who may be, or have been, political adversaries – as in the case of *The Demi-Paradise*, which deals with a Russian who visits Britain and finds he has misjudged the nation. Asquith's film sets out to forge links between the two cultures, while maintaining a distance on Russian 'otherness'. The split between self and other identified by Lusted is useful in drawing attention to the way discourses of national identity manage cultural difference.

National Fictions pays scant attention to anti-consensual voices, preferring to explore the parameters of consensus itself. Charles Barr's *All Our Yesterdays* makes a determined assault on the consensus (Barr, 1986). In it, Barr revises the position he took in *Ealing Studios* almost a decade before, arguing for a complete reworking of the terms in which British cinema is discussed. He demands more attention be given to the non-respectable 'underside' of our national cinema, but warns against the temptation to subscribe to a rigid opposition between realist and non-realist traditions. Instead, we need to hold together in the mind

> ... as 'British cinema', the modes of observation and interiority, of transparency and self-reflexivity, of sobriety and excess; Grierson and Loach, but also Powell and Hitchcock; and, in production and criticism alike, an instrumentalist indifference to the medium as such, but also a passionate interest in it (Barr, 1986, p. 24).

The importance of Barr's argument is that he sees these different strands as always interacting and interpenetrating: they are necessary to each other, even though the balance between them may shift. This gives a different inflection to the problem of British cinema's identity than the one offered by Julian Petley in 'The Lost Continent', which appears in the same book. Petley sees the dominance of a realist aesthetic in films and criticism as responsible for the way British cinema has been characterised as formally dull, lacking in style and auteurs. This leads him to posit the existence of a repressed, underground British cinema, in which he includes Hitchcock and Powell, and the Gainsborough melodramas. These films exist beneath the cultural surface, challenging the terms in which British cinema is normally conceived, which is why they have been critically ignored. Petley refers to John Ellis's article on the 40s project to create a British 'quality film' (Ellis, 1978), quoting his description of the latter as

> a unified and purposeful whole; it has the poetry and logic of a smooth flowing pattern; it controls the seduction of the photographic in the interests of a visual narrative; it adopts a restrained yet adult tone (Petley, 1986, p. 109).

Petley argues that the 'underground' films with which he is concerned define themselves against prevailing notions of quality. In fact, as I have argued elsewhere (Cook, 1983), in the case of the Gainsborough melodramas, even though the quality critics may have seen them as contravening criteria of realism and taste, the film-makers themselves saw the films as participating in the enterprise to produce a quality British cinema. The fact that they were box-office successes raises another question: how can they be described as 'underground' when they were popular at the time of their release (and still are, if attendances at the 1983 National Film Theatre season and the frequency with which the movies turn up on afternoon television are anything to go by)?

Petley's article operates a kind of reverse elitism in which the films he champions become canonised by virtue of their being in opposition to the established pantheon, when the situation is rather more complex. One wonders just how far this approach goes in genuinely redefining British cinema – indeed, it appears to end up confirming the quality consensus by depending so heavily on it. There is much at stake here: the overvaluing of critical discourse at the expense of audience response and the reclaiming of critically despised films for an alternative pantheon of the Romantic/Gothic smack of a distaste for commercialism and entertainment. This distaste surfaces in many of the responses garnered during the war years by Mass-Observation, whose diarists were predominantly middle-class (Richards and Sheridan, 1987). (Intriguingly, several of the responses show a deep distrust of cinema itself – not least as a 'germ-factory'.) This helps to illuminate how and why so many recent accounts of British cinema end up mirroring the 40s quality consensus, in spite of the writers' attempts to break it.

The suspicion of the popular, and the tendency to see it as the repository of reactionary or regressive ideologies, can be detected in other current discussions of national identity. It is there in the scathing irony with which Dawson and West in 'Our Finest Hour?' (Dawson and West, 1984) distance themselves from Churchillian and Thatcherite imperialist rhetoric and the epic adventure genre on which it rests. And it rears its head in the collection *Scotch Reels*, an investigation of nationalism and Scottish film culture (McArthur, 1982). In his introduction, Colin McArthur identifies the popular traditions of Tartanry and Kailyard as deformed and pathological expressions of Scottish national identity, announcing the intention of the book to interrogate and deconstruct those popular myths, which are inadequate to represent the reality of Scottish life. McArthur, like Dawson and West, distances himself from romantic nostalgia. He argues in another article in the same volume that Scottish film culture should reach outside itself to engage with Marxist and modernist discourses. He cites with approval the work of Syberberg, Bertolucci, Godard, Oshima, Snow, Straub/Huillet, Akerman, Rainer and Wollen/Mulvey.

Whatever the merits of McArthur's arguments in the Scottish context, his disassociation of himself from the popular and his alliance with a small group of avant-garde intellectuals evidences both cultural elitism and a profound unease with his own national identity. This inability to confront their implication in popular expressions of national identity afflicts many writers on the Left. In their desire to be pure, untainted by the slightest whiff of conservatism, they construct the popular as mediator of the ideologically impure. In so doing, they fail to come to terms with either the complexity of the popular and its imaginative appeal, or their own investment in traditional forms and myths – what Alison Light in *Forever England* (1991) calls 'the Tory in us all'.

McArthur's article usefully draws attention to three important aspects of national identity: one is the split between the self and other through which a nation constructs its own identity by 'fashioning the identity of the peoples on its periphery (and those it encountered in colonial conquests) in terms of a set of binary oppositions to the qualities it most celebrated in itself' (McArthur, 1982, p. 41). The second aspect is the importance of costume and decor in denoting Scottishness in cinema (although McArthur pays little attention to these factors in his analyses, which are primarily ideological). One of the most fascinating features of

Scotch Reels is its visual material, particularly the chapter by Murray Grigor, which traces the influence of the Maclan costume prints on visual representations of Scotland (Grigor, 1982). Third, a central part of McArthur's argument, and one which haunts most left writing on the subject, is the desire to find a more 'authentic' construction of national identity – one which will express the reality of contemporary Scottish life rather than appeal to a regressive, Romantic notion of a lost heroic past. The idea of hegemony developed in *National Fictions* seems effectively to scotch (!) this wish, since presumably the representation of national identity which achieves leadership by consent at any given moment is the most 'authentic' one, whether it represents reality accurately or not.

The critique of nostalgia is central to left discussion of national identity. The longing for an imaginary 'golden age' is often perceived to be embedded in the regressive myths of community from which traditional group and national identities are constructed. Such longings are generally seen as culturally conservative, obstructing the way to the

A lost heroic past: Richard Todd as *Rob Roy the Highland Rogue* (1953)

True or false: Liam Neeson in *Rob Roy*

formation of modern, progressive identities. It is rarely considered that nostalgia might play a productive role in national identity, releasing the desire for social change or resistance. The recent historical epic *Rob Roy* (Michael Caton-Jones, 1995), for example, recalls a turbulent moment in Scottish history when the clans, the cornerstone of Scotland's social system, were breaking apart. The elements of Tartanry and Kailyard dismissed by contributors to *Scotch Reels* (McArthur, 1982) are much in evidence: costume, music and landscape are used emotively to create a sense of the Scottish past as an arena for heroic action against social injustice.

This idealised version of history may appear to have little to do with 'reality', past or present; but the 'truth' of the past must surely change according to who perceives it. Rather than a refusal of nostalgia, it seems more pertinent to investigate the powerful emotional appeal of reliving the past and the part this plays in popular imaginings of community and resistance at specific historical moments. Yet the demand for truth in left analyses of fictional reconstructions of history is never far from the surface, even when, as in the case of *Rob Roy*, it is clear that the reconstruction is intended to work on the level of myth and legend. In an article for *Sight and Sound*, Liz Lochhead, while acknowledging her own pleasure in the epic, heroic qualities of the movie, feels compelled to distance herself:

> Of course we must dream on celluloid, but we need to dream more, different and varied dreams, to ask ourselves what truths about the present we are hiding from ourselves by lying about the past (Lochhead, 1995, p. 16).

In a chapter in his book on national identity and British cinema, *Waving the Flag*, Andrew Higson explores the historical context of Cecil Hepworth's 1923 film *Comin' Thro' the Rye* by investigating its contemporary critical reception (Higson, 1995). *Waving the Flag* is an impressive elaboration of Higson's earlier writings on national identity, situating his work within a broad tradition of left intellectual discussion of the subject. Higson distances himself from what he calls the 'orthodox history of British cinema' which 'identifies a select series of relatively self-contained quality film movements to carry forward the banner of national cinema' (Higson, 1995, p. 22). He takes to task those 'mainstream critics' who fail to face up to 'the actual differences and discontinuities which run across British film culture' (Higson, 1995, p. 23). Quoting from Michel Foucault's *The Archaeology of Knowledge* (Foucault, 1974), Higson argues for the unsettling of ready-made categories and groupings: 'The tranquillity with which they are accepted must be disturbed' (Higson, 1995, p. 23).

In his detailed analysis of *Comin' Thro' the Rye*, Higson places it within a relatively new category – that of the English 'heritage' film – setting out to demonstrate how Hepworth's movie celebrated a 'nostalgic pastoralism' (Higson, 1995, p. 44) in an attempt to create a version of English cultural heritage which would help to differentiate a quality British cinema from Hollywood. Among other distinctive features, Higson identifies a tension between narrative and image in *Comin' Thro' the Rye*: while the narrative depicted a decaying social order in late Victorian England, the images presented the past as spectacular display, timeless and unchanging:

> This version of the national past, this version of history, in which a critical perspective is displaced by decoration and display, 'an obsessive accumulation of comfortably archival detail', is not in any way confined to cinema: it is the very substance of the heritage industry and its

commodification, idealisation and marketing of the past (Higson, 1995, pp. 46–7).

Despite the fact that Higson includes a footnote to the effect that 'it would be wrong to assume that pastoral and nostalgic discourses are always conservative' (Higson, 1995, p. 47), his own critique of *Comin' Thro' the Rye* betrays a suspicion of the part played by nostalgia in the formation of national identity. Far from playing a positive role, nostalgia, associated with the spectacular display of period detail and thus contaminated by commodity fetishism, gets in the way of a more authentic critical approach to the national past. Ironically, this critique of the commodity status of cinematic images echoes the traditional supporters of quality British cinema against which Higson defines himself – see, for example, Ralph Bond (1945), quoted in Lant, 1991, p. 29. The idea that nostalgia, and indeed fetishism, might provide ways of actively engaging in the process of reconstructing the past, rather than simply encouraging 'passive' consumption of it, is generally not entertained by left commentators on 'heritage' cinema.

One of the questions hovering around recent work on cinema and

Heritage on display: *Comin' Thro' the Rye*

national identity is that of gender and sexuality. In *Scotch Reels* (McArthur, 1982) there is a submerged problem in the strident distaste for the decorative excesses of Tartanry and the sentimental, tear-jerking mechanisms of Kailyard. I do not need to stress the fact that both these characteristics are traditionally held to be 'feminine' while all the contributors to *Scotch Reels* are male. In *National Fictions* (Hurd, 1984), on the other hand, the question is raised more directly. Several articles point to the fact that, in spite of dramatic changes in the position of women during the war, the consensus films tend to portray them in traditional terms as wives and mothers, and primarily in domestic contexts. Others identify key moments in which (hetero)sexual desire threatens to transgress the boundaries of national identity (as in *The Demi-Paradise*).

In *Blackout: Reinventing Women for Wartime British Cinema*, Antonia Lant takes up where these writers leave off (Lant, 1991). Hers is the most extensive study to date of the relationship of women to the wartime consensus on national identity. She raids a variety of archival sources – films, cartoons, posters, advertisements – to demonstrate how the official project to construct national unity constantly stumbled over the uncertain, sliding nature of wartime femininity. Rather than looking for an authentic national identity for wartime women, Lant, in common with Alison Light in *Forever England* (Light, 1991), highlights the uncomfortable relationship of women to national identity itself.

Following other feminist commentators (for example, Harper, 1988), Lant stresses the fact that in 1939, women had been enfranchised citizens for only eleven years. This not only helps to account for their own precarious connection to citizenship and nationality, but suggests the deep ambivalence with which the state viewed their inclusion in the struggle for national unity. The situation was compounded by the extreme conditions of wartime, which meant that women's roles were rapidly changing, giving rise to a multiplicity of shifting definitions of femininity which resisted attempts to unify them. In the face of this gender slippage, Lant argues, official endeavours to address a unified female national subject were doomed to failure, and were marked by confusion and strain.

Blackout traces these ideological tangles through a number of texts in an attempt to establish a 'genre of the national subject', so called because it addressed 'a subject nationally defined' (Lant, 1991, p. 13). For the most part, Lant sees this genre epitomised in the critically sanctioned consensus films, and it is a weakness in her argument, as in others, that she chooses to concentrate on that small group of home-front films which more or less subscribed to official concepts of British cinema. The status of this handful of movies as a genre is immediately brought into question by the existence of a vast body of excluded work which also addressed audiences as national subjects at war. More extraordinary is the way Lant confirms the consensus by relegating the Gainsborough costume melodramas to the margins of her discussion, despite the existence of feminist work suggesting their aberrant qualities (Cook, 1983; Harper, 1983, 1988; Aspinall, 1983). *The Wicked Lady* (Leslie Arliss, 1945) makes a couple of brief appearances, but on the whole Lant neglects both films and arguments which might challenge her narrow focus. The result, once again, is a singularly lop-sided view of national identity.

Lant follows other work in the area in seeing British national identity as formed through a process of establishing difference from other, non-British identities, and she sees the USA as the primary 'other' from which British cinema differentiated itself during the war. This suits her case well, since the realist home-front movies did indeed so define themselves. The wartime debates about British cinema often adopted an anti-Hollywood stance, eschewing artificiality, glamour and naive propaganda in favour of realism, expressed in terms of 'truth', 'simplicity' and 'sincerity'. Britain's authentic national cinema, it was argued, should be concerned with specifically British subject-matter, concentrate on ordinary people leading everyday lives and adopt an aesthetic of restraint. Lant shows how the influence of the 30s documentary movement penetrated fiction films during the war, affecting them at every level, from subject matter and iconography to narrative construction.

One important consequence of the anti-Hollywood position was the central part played in the consensus films by de-glamorised British heroines, whose down-to-earth ordinariness was depicted as essential to national unity. Some films provided an ironic commentary on this imperative – *Perfect Strangers* (Alexander Korda, 1945), for instance, built its narrative around the glamorisation of its hero and heroine by the demands of wartime. (It is surely no coincidence that Korda had been one of the most vocal advocates during the 30s for an international British cinema which could compete with Hollywood on its own terms.) The deglamorised heroine of wartime British cinema was also a response to real economic conditions. Restrictions on glamour and fashion began in June 1941 with clothes rationing, and in 1942 the Civilian Clothing Order, which dressed the entire nation in utility clothing, was introduced.

This egalitarian move levelled off class, ethnic and gender differences,

30

Reflecting the national interest: Robert Donat and Deborah Kerr in *Perfect Strangers*

uniforming everyone in order to maintain national cohesion. At the same time, the sexualised, feminine woman was seen as a social threat, particularly to national security, and Lant provides numerous examples of the depiction of female sexuality as the enemy's greatest weapon. Other feminists (Modleski, 1991) have argued that war activates a particularly intense gender crisis which provokes the male, assailed by fears of annihilation, to identify woman, or femininity itself as the enemy. One could speculate, then, that war produces an impulse to masculinise culture – as a response to the threat of being 'swallowed up', whether by alien cultures or sexualities – and a consequent devaluation of the feminine.

Lant's work offers substantial evidence for this idea. The compulsory clothing regulations, which banned all decorative flourishes, affected women's clothing above all, bringing it closer to male attire. Cosmetics – a crucial factor in defining gender since the late 18th century's Great Masculine Renunciation, in which men abandoned their claim to be beautiful – were also subject to restrictions. War conditions created

31

mobile women who could be called on to take men's place in a variety of arenas: the Land Army and the women's armed services put women in uniforms that empowered their wearers by masculinising them. This erosion of sexual difference carried with it its own problems of con- tamination – identity, after all, depends upon the existence of an Other, negatively defined. The government took steps to ensure that decorative femininity was not totally erased. Labyrinthine legislation both con- trolled and protected the use of cosmetics, while the War Office, concerned that uniforms made women look just like men, commissioned corset designs from Berlei that would 'preserve the feminine line' while being practical underneath a uniform (Lant, 1991, p. 110). Such measures were designed to guarantee that a potentially disruptive notion of femininity as the repository of forbidden desires for decorative excess was managed and controlled, while remaining available for propaganda purposes to be mobilised as transgressive.

The mobile woman, while being essential to the home-front war effort, also threatened the official discourse of national unity, which depended on a traditional notion of women's place being in the home. This contradiction gave rise to anxieties which surface in some films in uncertainties of address. Lant's lengthy analysis of *The Gentle Sex* (Leslie Howard and Maurice Elvey, 1943) illuminates many of these anxieties and the strategies used to resolve them – the major device being Leslie Howard's framing presence as male observer and the use of his control- ling voice-over (Lant, 1991, pp. 80–98). Even here, Lant discerns hesitation and confusion in the project to 'manage' wartime gender disturbance.

The crisis of sexual identity precipitated by the war left indelible marks on the official attempts to project national unity. Lant's work is extremely suggestive about the centrality of gender crisis to discourses of national identity (something which previous work in the area had recognised but marginalised), and the way this works to disrupt any notion that cinema (or other cultural forms) relays such discourses unproblematically. Her readings of films, while choosing to remain within the limits of the consensus, test those limits to the point of breaking it open, revealing the impossibility of the project. Her emphasis on the importance of clothes and cross-dressing to the management of sexual and national identity is also provocative, although she does not integrate these insights into a theory of identity.

If Lant demonstrates the inconsistencies – even hysteria – inherent in wartime attempts to construct a coherent British national identity and an authentic national cinema, Alison Light, also a feminist historian, approaches the subject from the perspective of women themselves (Light, 1991). Although her discussion concentrates on literature of the 20s and 30s, she sees the formations of national character during this period as feeding directly into the Second World War. Between the wars, changes in Britain's national identity led to a cultural feminisation in which boundaries of class and gender were significantly shifted, producing irreversible changes in women's lives. Light looks at the work of female writers of the time for the ways in which they negotiate these changes, expressing conflict and resistance. A major part of her argument is the need for cultural historians on the Left to produce more personal histories which come to terms with subjectivity, recognising the interpenetration of private and public events. But more than this, she calls on them to acknowledge that conservatism – with a small 'c' – is not sealed off from other, conflicting ideologies or beliefs:

> In my view, those who believe themselves to be partisans drawn to very different political philosophies have a special responsibility to discover not where conservatism seems to us most strange, but, which is harder, to find out where it touches us most nearly – how best to understand the Tory in us all (Light, 1991, p. 18).

Light's book is a major intervention in discussions of national identity, which, as we have seen, often manifest symptoms of extreme discomfort with the whole idea in male writers on the Left because of its conservative connotations. Significantly, Light finishes her introduction on an elegiac note, claiming that the 'finest hour' version of Englishness no longer carries any authority, and giving space to her own sense of loss as someone whose childhood was inevitably coloured by its rhetoric. For Light, the aftermath of the First World War brought about an anti-heroic mood in Britain which caused a revolt against the romantic languages of national pride. This in turn produced a realignment of sexual identities which was part of a process of redefining Englishness:

> ... the 1920s and 30s saw a move a way from formerly heroic and officially masculine public rhetorics of national destiny and from a dynamic and missionary view of the Victorian and Edwardian middle classes in 'Great Britain' to an Englishness at once less imperial and more inward-looking, more domestic and more private – and, in terms of pre-war standards, more 'feminine' (Light, 1991, p. 8).

33

This profound shift in self-image culminated in the Second World War's focus on the home front and the heroic actions of 'ordinary people'. Light points out that in spite of the domestication of British culture between the wars, literary histories of the period pay scant attention to 'home', and to feelings of belonging, preferring to concentrate on the work of those male writers who rejected what they saw as a safe, smug Britain and looked abroad to foreign cultures for challenge and stimulus: 'Abroad was culture, romance and sensuality; home was philistine, prosaic and frigid. 'Home' was also the place where women were, after 1919, in the majority and where women writers were coming into their own' (Light, 1991, p. 7). If these changes produced phobic reactions in male writers to the suburbanisation of Britain (symptomatic of the fear of being 'swallowed up' already noted as haunting national identity), for women they heralded new freedoms and cultural opportunities, which led to a rebellion against pre-1918 ideas of domesticity. Thus, while masculinity and ideas of the nation were being 'feminised', 'the feminine' was also being radically recast, as were class identities.

Light examines the work of middlebrow women writers popular between the wars for the ways in which it expresses and comments on these identity crises. She sees the vogue for thrillers, for instance, as a manifestation of an obsession with disguise and deceit in the face of increasing difficulties in discerning 'who was who'. Unlike most other critics, she finds in Agatha Christie an ironic distance on traditional English xenophobia. The Belgian detective Hercule Poirot frequently mocks English insularity. Light quotes a characteristic passage from *Three Act Tragedy* (1935) in which he turns the tables: 'To speak the broken English is an enormous asset. It leads people to despise you. They say – a foreigner – he can't even speak English properly. ... And so, you see, I put people off their guard' (Light, 1991, p. 85).

This quote finds an echo in an anecdote in Karol Kulik's biography of Alexander Korda, himself frequently the victim of English xenophobia and anti-semitism. Kulik cites a passage from R. C. Sherriff's autobiography in which he refers to Korda's Hungarian accent:

I once asked him how he managed to get so much money out of the hard-headed, tight-fisted financiers in the city when our own native film producers couldn't raise a penny out of them. He waved the question aside with a modest little smile, and said, 'It is easy. You ask for it in broken English' (Kulik, 1975, p. 162).

34

Both these instances reveal a contradiction at the heart of xenophobia: the desire to insist on the superiority of the British is matched by an equal and opposite desire to submit to the 'foreign'.

For Light, Jan Struther's 'Mrs Miniver' columns written for *The Times* at the end of the 30s are most revealing of the new British national identity she describes. The MGM film version (William Wyler, 1942) was seen as one of the most effective pieces of propaganda for Britain since the war began, and Churchill maintained that Mrs Miniver did more for the Allied cause than a flotilla of battleships. Yet the values celebrated in the genteel musings of this upper-middle-class woman seem aeons away from the Churchillian rhetoric of national pride. In fact, the 'Mrs Miniver' columns leading up to 1939 were internationalist and anti-fascist rather than nationalist, and dedicated to an idea of the national character as peaceful and home-loving. Light analyses differences between *The Times* columns and the film, showing how the romantic Toryism of the Churchillian mood built on the conservatism of appeasement characteristic of the former to transform it into a powerful new sense of national history ' ... not as the doings of the great and the good, but as that which was made by the little, ordinary people at home, "muddling through"' (Light, 1991, p. 154). This 'little England', evoking a patriotism of private life, was captured in the 1939 popular song 'There'll Always Be an England' sung by Vera Lynn, celebrating an understated, intimate national spirit at odds with the bombast of 'Rule Britannia'.

Light's discussion of the domesticated version of British national identity which emerged between the wars clarifies many of the underlying assumptions of the drive to produce a particular kind of understated, realist national cinema during the 40s. It also helps in understanding the overwhelming emphasis on the home front in the Second World War, and the consequent focus on women's experiences, which also fed into cinema, particularly into the contemporary home-front movies. When we come to Light's chapter on Daphne Du Maurier, we find the other side of this home-centred ethic. Here is another identity, restless and searching for ways to escape the trap of domesticity, indeed, of femininity itself, which fed just as effectively into wartime national identity, though it had little voice in the consensus except as a negative pole against which to judge 'positive' femininity.

Light describes Du Maurier's work as 'a romance with the past' – a past conceived as a place of excitement and desire in contrast to a lacklustre present (Light, 1991, p. 156). Smugglers, pirates and gypsies are her heroes, and her heroines identify with the transgressive male characters. Du Maurier herself often chose to write in the first person singular, masculine gender, and wrote 'like a man', in visceral, violent prose which went against the grain of the women's romantic novel. Du Maurier's debt was rather to the adventure stories of Robert Louis Stevenson. She celebrated a swashbuckling masculinity which looked back to a *Boys' Own* version of the past, while clearly being aware that such images of masculinity were no longer viable in the post-war context. Thus the manliness of her heroes was as much in doubt as the femininity of her heroines.

For Light, Du Maurier's novels manifest a desire to be differently female, to break free from the confines of home and family, to be 'a vagrant on the face of the earth' (Light, 1991, p. 166). This is romantic, escapist literature of the kind that inspired the Gainsborough costume dramas – indeed, 'escapist' was the term used derogatively to describe those films. That they should be derided in these terms indicates both the strength of the 'reality principle' operating in discourses of national cinema at that time, and also the threat posed to ideologies of national unity by the very idea of escape. Du Maurier, born into a theatrical family of immigrants, also transgresses national boundaries in her dramatisation in stories such as *Frenchman's Creek* (1941) and *My Cousin Rachel* (1951) of the English romance with 'foreign' sexuality – the desire for the Other which underlies xenophobia.

Light's interrogation of women's literature between the wars demonstrates how uneasy many women were with their place in discourses of national identity. The emphasis on house and home produced a desire to redefine femininity, giving rise to conflicting and resistant arguments, many of which survived into the Second World War. Most pertinent to my own discussion of national identity is her conclusion that identity is an unstable, shifting category which she likens both to an ill-fitting costume and a temporary, nomadic dwelling (Light, 1991, p. 221). The ambivalence towards home, the vagrant desire to contravene national boundaries, could perhaps form the basis of a different concept of national identity, and national cinema.

In a chapter entitled 'How English Is It?' in his book *Sentimental Education*, James Donald also reflects on the importance of 'home' to ideas of national culture, quoting both Edward Said and Benedict Anderson to the effect that 'the nation' is a symbolic universe to which we feel we belong (Donald, 1992, p. 50). Nationhood implies a place where we feel at home, though it does not necessarily depend on the territorial existence

36

of a nation state. The main thrust of Donald's argument is about the role of popular literature in sustaining nationality and race, and he proposes the concept of *bricolage* – the activity of combination and recombination – to explain the transgressive process of reading. He likens this process to furnishing a rented apartment with our own acts, memories and designs, making a temporary accommodation habitable. This suggests a vagrant spirit at work in reading, which recalls Alison Light's definition of identity (Light, 1991). And, indeed, Donald cites Michel de Certeau: 'Readers are like travellers; they move across lands belonging to someone else, like nomads poaching their way across fields they did not write ' (Donald, 1992, p. 59).

Donald draws on the work of Peter Stallybrass and Allon White in *The Politics and Poetics of Transgression* to illuminate the processes of identity formation (Stallybrass and White, 1986). Collective identity depends on the construction of boundaries which mark the difference between a social group and those it must exclude in order to maintain its unity and coherence. These borders between self and other, inside and outside, are, however, insecure, permeable. The 'inside' is always fragmented and differentiated rather than pure and united, and the 'others' are never successfully expelled. The act of exclusion produces symptoms: the 'others' return in the form of grotesques to haunt the official culture. The struggle to oust this grotesque produces another, which can be described as 'a boundary phenomenon of hybridisation or inmixing, in which self and other become enmeshed in an inclusive, heterogeneous, dangerously unstable zone' (Donald, 1992, p. 58). This complex, hybrid fantasy emerges from the very attempt to demarcate boundaries.

As Donald points out, this play of identity and otherness helps to explain the ambivalent repugnance and fascination evident in representations of the grotesque Other. But it is also useful in shedding light on the part played by desire in identity formation. The play between expulsion and return suggests that the impulse to purify and unify hinges on the wish to be swallowed up, penetrated or invaded – that each is necessary to the other. Thus boundaries are erogenous zones where identities are formed and, crucially, lost. Donald quotes a passage from Sax Rohmer's *The Mystery of Dr Fu Manchu* to illustrate the split in identity which, as Edward Said argues in *Orientalism*, enabled European culture to create the Orient as an 'underground self' (Donald, 1992, p. 59). Following Stallybrass and White, Donald sees this split in identity as 'the ground of racial difference' (Donald, 1992, p. 60). He fails to note, however, the sexual ambivalence at work in Rohmer's descriptions of Fu Manchu – the alien's feline qualities, and the imagery of invasive mists and aromas which characterise his threat to the 'upright' British policeman Nayland Smith. Fu Manchu's 'foreignness' is intimately linked with his 'femininity'; both are seen as contaminating, viral forces which respect no borders, positions or rules.

Donald's discussion of identity formation leads him to Freud's account of the basic instability of the ego itself and its acting out in fantasy or reverie. In the essay 'A Child Is Being Beaten' (Freud, 1979), Freud stresses the mobility of sexual identity in fantasy, the oscillation of the subject between multiple positions of identification, including those of 'masculine' and 'feminine'. This is the basis of the figure of the double which appears in popular fiction. Donald's example is Robert Louis Stevenson's *The Strange Case of Dr Jekyll and Mr Hyde*, in which the relationship between the rational scientist and his monstrous other self oscillates between the poles masculine (reason) and feminine (animal, perversion, hysteria). Donald is careful not to attribute any 'progressive' motivation or effect to popular fiction's working through of problems of identity; indeed, the narrative drive of these fantasies seems to be towards the demarcation of unity, order and wholeness: 'The social function of such mass circulation scenarios, the institution of popular fiction, thus seems to be both to enunciate the restlessness of desire and the unreliability of symbolic boundaries, and yet to give them some stability' (Donald, 1992, p. 64).

However, it is important to remember that the operations of desire seem to require the transgression of boundaries of sexual identity. Depending on the emphasis the reader wishes to give to either transgression or stabilisation, popular fiction can be seen as either disrupting or reaffirming traditional norms. Donald's formulation thus goes some way towards shifting the 'low' popular/'high' modernist dichotomy found in much discussion of national identity (see, for example, *Scotch Reels*, McArthur, 1982).

Donald's closing remarks are also suggestive for my own argument. Referring to the 'English garden' effect, he describes the way 'the national culture' is produced through establishing the nation as 'an imaginary landscape of everyday life' which has 'the required air of naturalness, pathos and hope' (Donald, 1992, p. 69). This evocative image strongly recalls the neat, suburban garden surrounding Ealing Studios' 'home', and the terms in which the desire for a British cinema which is truthful, sincere and realistic has so often been formulated. The image takes on added poignancy when it is considered that the 'English garden' effect redesigns the landscape of the homeland to efface the signs of past atrocities. Thus the culture where we feel at home, though it may appear *heimlich*, is rendered *unheimlich* (uncanny). 'Home' is, in fact, a haunted house.

My journey through some of the key writings on British cinema and national identity has led me far away from the apparent certainties of the wartime project to produce a national cinema with clear national boundaries and a coherent, fixed identity. Indeed, I have come face to face with the impossibility of unified, coherent identities, and with the ghosts shadowing the official attempts to solidify cultural differences and linguistic variations into the nation state. However, I do not mean to imply that the categories of national cinema and national identity can or should therefore be dissolved, or rejected. As Alison Light (1991) has pointed out, the rejection of 'home' in favour of exile can be problematic, as in the case of those male writers between the wars who denounced a 'domesticated' Britain and sought exoticism abroad. There are, of course, many ways in which the idea of national culture can be recast to accommodate diversity – by differentiating between local ethnic communities rather than incorporating them into 'Englishness', for example. But it is also a question of recasting identity itself.

The instability at the core of identity, and the unease attendant upon notions of 'home', produce symptoms, or leaks in the system which point to the permeability of the boundaries delimiting identity. (The importance of boundary areas is clear from the way they are so heavily policed. The Berlin Wall was a prime example of the impossibility of plugging 'leaks' in the borders of national identity.) This permeability is rarely taken into account in discussions of national identity and British cinema, which tend to work within a consensus which accepts the limits of national borders, even when they explore those limits. The result has been a narrow, closed definition of British cinema, which has contributed to the widely held view that it is parochial and cinematically unadventurous. The key to dissolving the consensus would seem to lie in breaking away from the centre, where the categories of identity wield their authority, towards the edges, where that authority is always being tested. This enables a complex position to be taken up in relation to the home culture: neither simply 'inside', which would confirm its stability, nor simply 'outside', which would imply the refusal characteristic of exile, but both inside and outside at once.

The crossing and re-crossing of national boundaries makes travellers of us all. In his article 'Every Time We Say Goodbye', John Berger argues that cinema, unlike theatre, painting or literature, is the art of travelling. It transports us elsewhere, to different times and places, enabling us to inhabit and be inhabited by different selves:

> What is saved in the cinema when it achieves art is a spontaneous continuity with all of mankind. It is not an art of the princes or of the bourgeoisie. It is popular and vagrant. In the sky of the cinema people learn what they might have been and discover what belongs to them apart from their single lives (Berger, 1991, p. 17).

We might wish to question the extent to which cinema stands alone among the arts in offering the delights of wandering. But it is this vagrant spirit, seeking encounters with other, alien identities, which has been singularly lacking in discussions of British cinema – though not in British cinema itself, as I hope to show in my examination of Gainsborough costume dramas. To introduce the idea of the critic/reader/viewer as itinerant is to transform our national cinema and the way it has previously been understood. The question 'Where do we go from here?' takes on new meaning.

III

CHANGING PLACES:
COSTUME AND IDENTITY

Costume design is one of the most under-researched areas of cinema history. A vast amount of literature exists on theatrical costume and, since the 70s, there has been a burgeoning of interest in fashion among cultural historians; to all this, film studies has, for the most part, remained impervious. There are some obvious reasons for the neglect: the importance accorded the director at the expense of other contributors to 'the look' of the finished product, and the domination of 70s film theory by narrative analysis and literary notions of 'the text', for example. The lack of interest in costume becomes particularly remarkable when one considers how important clothes are to narrative, in establishing character, in reinforcing plot, in suggesting mood and so forth. While the age of the great Hollywood designers – Adrian, Walter Plunkett, Travis Banton, Edith Head *et al.* – may be over, the costume designer still occupies a key place in the screen credits, up there in front with the cinematographer, the screenwriter, the production designer and editor (all of whom, it must be said, have received more attention from historians). *Fabrications*, a book attempting to theorise costume from a feminist perspective, includes in its bibliography a conspicuously short section concerning costume on the screen and a noticeably long section entitled 'Feminism and Cultural Studies' (Gaines and Herzog, 1990). It represents the first sustained endeavour to bring the insights of the latter to bear on the former.

The marginalisation of costume design by film theorists is marked enough to be diagnosed as a symptom. Indeed, costume and its sister fashion as areas of study share some of the attributes identified in relation to national identity in the previous section – not surprising, perhaps, since costume plays an important part in asserting and reinforcing national identity. (The political power of national dress can be deduced from historical attempts to suppress it – as when the English prohibited the Irish in the 16th century and the Scots in the 18th century from wearing their traditional costume.) There is in critical approaches to costume and fashion both ambivalence and a consensus of opinion which is beginning to tear at the seams, revealing what was also exposed in my journey through the terrain of national identity: the instability of identity itself.

A witty and evocative essay by Umberto Eco – included (appropriately enough, since it allows me to pick up the motif of the itinerant critic) in *Faith in Fakes: Travels in Hyperreality* – encapsulates in one short piece many of the anxieties hovering around approaches to costume (Eco, 1995). In 'Lumbar Thought', Eco describes the experience of wearing jeans again after a long period during which weight problems forced him to renounce this pleasure. The jeans made their presence felt, closely gripping the lower half of his body and causing him to move differently – they 'imposed a demeanour' (Eco, 1995, p. 193) on him. Consultants of the opposite sex confirmed what the philosopher had already suspected: 'That for women experiences of this kind are familiar because all their garments are conceived to impose a demeanour – high heels, girdles, brassieres, pantyhose, tight sweaters' (Eco, 1995, p. 192). Eco goes on to speculate how different the history of civilisation might be if the constraints of costume were loosened; if Freud had been a Scotsman wearing a kilt, 'under which, as everyone knows, the rule is to wear nothing' (Eco, 1995, p. 193), would he have described Oedipal triangles in the same way? For Eco, the restricting jeans, by focusing his attention on demeanour, reduced his capacity for interior reflection, forcing him towards exterior life through 'epidermic self-awareness' (Eco, 1995, p. 194).

This leads him to the conclusion that thought, in the sense of philosophical rumination, depends upon the body being left completely free and unaware of itself. Throughout the centuries, thinkers have been dressed in loose, flowing garments which enabled them to ignore their bodies and develop their interior lives: 'Thought abhors tights' (Eco, 1995, p. 194). Returning to the question of women, Eco reflects that their 'enslavement to fashion' not only made them sex objects, but compelled them to live for the exterior: 'And this makes us realise how intellectually gifted and heroic a girl had to be before she could become, in those clothes, Madame de Sévigné, Vittoria Colonna, Madame Curie, or Rosa Luxemburg' (Eco, 1995, p. 194). Thus jeans, far from being a symbol of female emancipation and equality with men, imprison the body and so restrict thought. Finally, Eco warns, fashion is a language which, like other forms of communication, influences our view of the world, but in a far more physical way. His experience of wearing jeans has taught him – 'via the groin' – that 'the dialectic between oppression and liberation, and the struggle to bring light' follows many mysterious paths (Eco, 1995, p. 195).

Eco's article revolves around a number of recurring motifs in cultural analysis of fashion. First, there is an anxiety about the body. The philosopher's overweight body is out of control – the tight jeans squeeze it into shape, re-form, or de-form it. This, however, leads to further anxiety: the restricting jeans prevent thought; the body is better left unfettered and ignored, in its 'natural' state. Second, there is unease about boundaries: between interior and exterior, self and other, body and mind. Clothes mark the threshold between the body and the outside world, between the private and the public. They can hide or reveal, but either way they expose our vulnerability. Fashion, which requires a style statement, compounds the problem. It is both self-expression and social pressure, compelling us to conform. Fashion dictates identity – in Eco's terms, 'imposes a demeanour' on us. Even worse, it is responsible for the oppression of women, who, enslaved by the need to appear attractive, find it difficult to think. Fashion is inimical to thought: it is irrational.

Third, there are misgivings about identity itself. Does it reside inside, in the mind, or outside, on the body? Eco's jeans cause a shift, even a crisis, in identity. He is no longer the absent-minded professor, but the social critic. He entertains anarchic and iconoclastic fantasies: what if Freud had been a Scotsman (how's that for identity crisis)? The jeans make a transvestite of him; he identifies strongly with oppressed womankind. Finally, Eco voices one of the most widely held resistances to fashion. Clothes, like language, are a semiotic system. Language is arbitrary, so clothes are not to be trusted. The jeans, though they may appear to be a symbol of emancipation, are in fact 'a trap of domination' (Eco, 1995, p. 194).

The conundrums crossing Eco's playful article echo through the history of costume, from the nineteenth-century dress reform movements to the controversy surrounding the New Look in post-war Britain. The ambivalence noted above, combined with others – such as suspicion of fashion's contamination by consumerism and elitism – have contributed to the silence surrounding screen costume. It would be easy to argue, too, that the subject is seen as unworthy of study because it belongs to the female domain. Certainly, many costume designers and supervisors are

43

women; it is one of the few areas in film-making where women have consistently been able to make their mark. And it is true that what is perceived as feminine is often rendered trivial. However, there is more to it than that.

For a start, many of the aforementioned anxieties surface in feminist approaches to fashion. It is no coincidence that Eco, writing in 1976 at the height of the feminist revival, aligns himself with women 'enslaved' by fashion. Feminist film theory, with its distrust of spectacle and of a female body cut to the measure of male desire, echoed these qualms, and must bear some of the responsibility for perpetuating an aversion to costume defined in terms of fetishism and voyeurism. It is not simply a question of drawing attention to a neglected area of female endeavour, of rewriting history. What is at stake are competing definitions of femininity itself: woman as slave or mistress of her own and others' destiny, or both; femininity as artifice and construct or authenticity, or both; woman to be looked at, or looking, or both; femininity as stability, or oscillation.

It is the slipperiness of fashion, its very unpredictability, that disconcerts. Fashion is synonymous with change; it constantly reworks the past in a frenzied pursuit of the new. There is excitement and erotic charge in the way it constantly challenges the frontiers of the possible. Of course, this is the market place, so there is a price to pay – we are in the realms of commodity fetishism. But fashion is also cultural; it is an art form with something to say so it can resist, or comment on, its commodity status. Fashion's mutability is also resistant to 'rational' analysis and renders it slightly uncanny: clothes seem to have a life of their own. Elizabeth Wilson in *Adorned in Dreams* puts this eeriness down to the fact that clothes are relics of the past – like ghosts, they linger on after their wearers are dead (Wilson, 1985). But it may also have something to do with what they tell us about identity. Clothes are like doubles: they remind us that we are not unique.

Wilson's lively polemic on behalf of fashion is a history not only of costume but of social and cultural attitudes towards it. She challenges the consensus which sees fashion as corrupt, tainted by consumerism or imposing false identities. Instead, she argues that it should be seen as a complex aesthetic medium for the expression of ideas, beliefs and desires circulating in society. Like other cultural artefacts, fashion resolves at the imaginary level social contradictions that cannot be resolved (Wilson, 1985, p. 9). Wilson links fashion with the city and modernity in the way it plays out the tension between hedonism and repression in capitalist society. But its predilection for irony and paradox means that it comes into its own in the post-modernist epoch, when clashing styles can be used iconoclastically to question conventional ideals of beauty or design. Fashion articulates the problems of fragmentation, dislocation and alienation that modernity brings with it. The threat of self-annihilation endemic to modern city life is both recognised and refuted in fashion's pursuit of individual style. Wilson accepts that fashion is ambiguous – it can liberate or subjugate; but it is precisely this double-edged quality, its capacity to evade being pinned down to any one meaning or function, which she sees as its strength.

Crucially, for my own argument, Wilson's analysis characterises costume as crossing boundaries between different periods and locations. One of the charges commonly levelled at costume and fashion is their lack of authenticity. They pillage the past and other national styles in a constant activity of *bricolage*, emptying period and place of their original meanings and recombining them into new, vulgarised configurations. However, this is not just cultural imperialism or retrograde nostalgia. Fashion's appropriations are also a resistance to purity. They express a complex relationship with other cultures and other times: a desire to 'be' someone else, somewhere else – in fact, to be 'other'. They project the self as a hybrid amalgam of 'others', and in doing so, flirt with the loss of self. (Costume is rarely authentic: Wilson points out that even national dress, which is supposed to represent unique cultural values, is a mixed bag of cross-cultural borrowings.)

Fashion's capacity for holding multiple ideas in play is characteristic of fetishism. In some very obvious ways, fetishism plays a large part in the pleasure we get from fashion, from tight-lacing bondage games to the erotic charge given off by shiny silks and satins or leather. Less obviously, it motivates our desire to possess exquisite objects which we endow with magical properties: the Versace print shirt, the Lacroix jacket, the Nicole Fahri shoes. Freud's description of fetishism (Freud, 1977b) characterises it as originating in the (male) child's fear of castration on seeing his mother's genitals. The absence of the penis he believed her to possess provokes a compromise reaction in which 'something else' – an object – absorbs all the interest which formerly belonged to the penis. Because of its foundation in the sight of the female body, and its consequent repression of the 'knowledge' which that look imparts, fetishism has been much discussed by feminist theory. Laura Mulvey's influential 'Visual Pleasure' article (Mulvey, 1989a) provoked a debate in film studies which continues today.

I do not have space here to go into these arguments, or into the shortcomings of Freud's formulation, which, as Linda Williams points out in *Hard Core*, seems to subscribe to the very misrecognition of female sexuality he identifies in the fetishist (Williams, 1990, p. 105). Suffice it to say that feminist critiques of fetishism, in their anxiety to dislodge the fetishist's phallocentrism (in his denial of female 'lack', he sees the penis everywhere), have adopted a somewhat moralistic and monolithic line. Fetishism has often been seen as an exclusively male perversion which entirely circumscribes and defines female sexuality, projecting an illusory, imaginary figment of the woman's body, which bears no relationship to true, 'authentic' femininity. This formulation ignores both the labile quality of fetishism (implicit in Freud's definition) and the fact that women can be fetishists (also ignored by Freud).

At the heart of Freud's idea of fetishism lies the notion that the phallus – signifier of power and difference – is detachable; in this sense, everyone can possess it, in fantasy, at least. This might be taken to confirm phallocentricity; but because, in Freud's view, the fetish is not just a phallic substitute but retains the indelible marks of the 'knowledge' of lack it attempts to repress, fetishism is better seen in terms of oscillation between a number of intersecting categories: knowledge and illusion, lack and plenitude, power and impotence. The fetishist's misrecognition on which feminists have laid so much emphasis is inextricable from the recognition which inspired it. 'I know, but ...' is the phrase which encapsulates the fetishist's ability to embrace several conflicting ideas simultaneously – thus fetishism traverses the boundary between truth and fiction, natural and artificial, calling into question essentialist categories of gender.

The crisis of gender category articulated by fetishism is relevant to my discussion of cross-dressing below. For the moment I want to suggest that the concept of fetishism, which, particularly in its Marxist sense of 'commodity fetishism', has traditionally been used to condemn fashion and costume for their impurity, can instead be employed to illuminate the ways in which our erotic obsessions with clothes are also transgressive in their play with identity and identification. Identification is another area which has been perceived in a limiting manner by film theory, with consequences for discussion of screen costume. Charles Eckert's magisterial study of the system of consumer tie-ins in operation in 20s and 30s Hollywood is a case in point (Eckert, 1990). One cannot fail to be impressed by the panache and scholarly attention to detail with which Eckert lays out the merchandising strategies employed by the studio sales departments at the height of Hollywood's penetration of the US market place. His article remains a solitary attempt to theorise a phenomenon – cinema's influence on fashion – which is often remarked upon but seldom seriously addressed.

Yet one cannot avoid the feeling that Eckert's description of the Hollywood sales managers' ideal consumer as a young woman entirely under the spell of their manipulative methods reveals his own ambivalence towards women as the dupes of consumer culture, and towards popular cinema as its vehicle. For Eckert, identification is a seamless, unproblematic process whereby cinema spectators, wishing to be exactly like the glamorous stars they see on the screen, are compelled to purchase the commodities they are led to believe will help them achieve this. Fetishism, by eroticising products, plays an important part in identification. We are back in the territory of costume as promoting false consciousness. But Eckert's account has within it the seeds of another idea. His description of the young woman piecing together a 'look', or identity which is a composite of different star images suggests that what is at work here is less a perfect identification than a play with identity itself. Rather than simply being a stooge of consumerism, the female spectator becomes a kind of performance artist, putting on and taking off different roles. Clearly, this does not mean that she escapes consumerism altogether: successful marketing, as Eckert's analysis makes clear, depends upon just this kind of multiple identification. But she is, at least, both victim and appropriator, object and subject, instrument and agent.

Eckert's notion of identification as a passive, 'feminine' submission to a regime of images controlled by men finds a mirror reflection in feminist film theory which constructs Hollywood cinema's spectacular display of female bodies as the embodiment of male desire, enacted via the deployment of a sadistic, voyeuristic gaze. This position, first theorised in 1975 by Laura Mulvey (Mulvey, 1989a), sees the female form in classic Hollywood films as passive object of the male hero's controlling look. It also posits that the audience's look is channelled exclusively through the male protagonist's gaze at the fetishised body of the female star, so that all spectators are compelled to share masculine castration anxieties and defences against them. These arguments have been taken up and challenged elsewhere. For the moment, I want to focus on two aspects of Mulvey's richly textured article, which, in spite of its monolithic line on Hollywood, like Eckert's, contains the seeds of other possible positions. The first is display – the woman's 'to-be-looked-atness', and the second is audience identification.

Mulvey's analysis depends upon an active/looking, passive/looked-at split corresponding to a male-female gender divison. Display is seen as passive; it is simply a reflection of the male protagonist/spectator's obsessive anxieties focused on the female body. Thus, writing about Alfred Hitchcock's *Rear Window* (1954), Mulvey argues:

> Lisa's exhibitionism has already been established by her obsessive interest in dress and style, in being a passive image of visual perfection; Jeffries' voyeurism and activity have also been established through his work as a photo-journalist, a maker of stories and captor of images (Mulvey, 1989a, p. 16).

Tania Modleski, among others, has outlined the problems in this analysis (Modleski, 1988). It is striking that, in the interests of sustaining the active/passive gender division, Mulvey's description ignores both the active dimension of exhibitionism (Freud links scopophilia – pleasure in looking – to the exhibitionist's desire to get a look at others' genitals by displaying his own: Freud, 1977a, p. 70) and the passive dimension of voyeurism (the desire to be 'exposed', or found out). It is also clear that Lisa's role in the narrative of *Rear Window* is far from passive: she constantly strives to attract Jeffries' attention, to capture his look, entering into his fantasy and putting herself at risk – acting (standing in) for him.

The definition of display as passive sets up a number of blocks. It confirms its derogatory association with femininity (historically, since the Great Masculine Renunciation of the late 18th century, women's dress has been decorative and excessive, while men's has been sober and restrained). It reinforces the idea that costume simply reflects, or facilitates the objectification of women. (Significantly, though Mulvey hints at the importance of clothes and fabrics to cinematic fetishism, she 'looks through' costume to the female form, or body.) It minimises the extent to which display (and, by implication, femininity) is a troublesome phenomenon which intrudes on, rather than serves the interests of, the narrative. Mulvey alludes to, but does not develop, this point when she discusses the capacity of the eroticised female image to cause a temporary halt in narrative development (Mulvey, 1989a, p. 12). She sees these isolated moments as breaking the illusion of depth demanded by narrative in order to flatten the female image, to give it the quality of an icon. By contrast, the active male protagonist is a three-dimensional figure.

Mulvey's focus on the controlling power of directors such as Sternberg and Hitchcock also has the effect of eradicating the part played by costume (and art direction) in the 'look' of a film. It is interesting that Hitchcock insisted that costume should be kept in a subservient role of supporting rather than disrupting narrative (Gaines and Herzog, 1990) – particularly in the light of the ambivalence towards costume evident in many of his films. *Vertigo* (1958), for instance, associates costume with deception (clothes are not to be trusted), while *Rebecca* (1940) hinges on a drama of identity crisis in which the unnamed heroine puts on the dead Rebecca's gown, with disastrous consequences. Finally, before leaving Mulvey's discussion of display, I should note that it implies a hostility to glamour, which is reminiscent of the anti-Hollywood arguments which motivated debates about British cinema during the Second World War. Behind Mulvey's polemic lurks the familiar longing for an authentic femininity, cleansed of contamination by male fantasy.

For Mulvey, identification is crucial to the way narrative cinema neutralises the threat of disruption posed by the erotic spectacle of woman.

> This is made possible through the process set in motion by structuring the film around a main controlling figure with whom the spectator can identify. As the spectator identifies with the main male protagonist, he projects his look onto that of his like, his screen surrogate, so that the power of the male protagonist as he controls events coincides with the active power of the erotic look, both giving a satisfying sense of omnipotence. A male movie star's glamorous characteristics are thus not those of the erotic object of the gaze, but those of the more perfect, more complete, more powerful ideal ego conceived in the original moment of recognition in front of the mirror (Mulvey, 1989a, p. 12).

It has often been pointed out that this formulation is inadequate to describe the complexity of the identification process, and I have already discussed in the previous chapter an alternative view expressed in James Donald's article 'How English Is It?' (Donald, 1992). It is important to stress the multiple cross-identifications at work in fantasy, and, indeed, the many different identifications which make up the individual person-ality. But I am more interested here in the way Mulvey characterises narrative cinema as playing on a tension between the loss and reinforce-ment of the self:

> The cinema has structures of fascination strong enough to allow temporary loss of ego while simultaneously reinforcing the ego. The

sense of forgetting the world as the ego has subsequently come to perceive it (I forgot who I am and where I was) is nostalgically reminiscent of that pre-subjective moment of image recognition (Mulvey, 1989a, p. 10).

She goes on to stress the ways in which cinema reinforces the (male) ego. But a slightly different emphasis, on the relinquishing of individuality crucial to 'losing oneself' in narrative fictions, produces a different analysis: one which sees cinema as the site of playing out of shifts and ruptures in identity which are not necessarily so neatly or easily resolved. That we wish to forget who and where we are suggests that the desire to transgress the boundaries of the self is fundamental to identity. It is possible to see narrative cinema as offering a variety of disguises for the spectator to try on and discard – the errant pleasures of transvestism. This notion at least has the advantage of drawing attention to the importance of costume in the operations of cinema.

In a later, 1981 article, 'Afterthoughts on "Visual Pleasure and Narrative Cinema" inspired by King Vidor's *Duel in the Sun* (1946)' (Mulvey, 1989b), Mulvey takes on board some of the criticisms levelled at her earlier piece. Here, she discusses the female spectator's transsexual identification, the oscillation between active and passive positions characteristic, according to Freud, of femininity itself – though this oscillation remains dormant in the woman's achievement of the 'correct' passive feminine position. Mulvey refers to this female trans-sexual identification as a strait-jacket, in that it reactivates the pleasure of an earlier, active 'masculine' sexuality only to reinforce its repression. Thus Mulvey's position in 'Afterthoughts' is hardly less pessimistic about the possibility of representing the feminine in patriarchal society than that in 'Visual Pleasure'. Yet 'Afterthoughts' also contains the seeds of another argument, one that releases femininity from its strait-jacket. Referring to the transvestite pleasures of female fantasy, Mulvey suggests, but does not follow up, a role for femininity as agent of gender category crisis, in which the accepted definitions of 'masculine' and 'feminine' are thrown into disarray. This more positive interpretation of cross-dressing is elaborated by Marjorie Garber (Garber, 1992). But it is also important to note that in the film Mulvey chooses to analyse, *Duel in the Sun*, there is another kind of oscillation. Pearl Chavez's tragedy is not just one of frustrated tomboy desire but of racially mixed identities – of the impure and corrupted sacrificed to the pure and authentic.

Gaines and Herzog's *Fabrications* (1990) attempts to open up the area of screen costume, both in terms of legitimising it as a subject for study and moving the feminist debate on. In her introduction, Gaines points to the obsession with authenticity which characterises both the studies of costume historians and the way costume is designed for the movies. Historians have tended to focus on the inaccuracy of screen costume (for example, Maeder, 1987), while the studios spent fortunes on research to get every detail of the designs correct. Since costume is a heterogeneous amalgam of styles and period anyway, the quest for exactitude would appear to be a lost cause. Nevertheless, it illuminates the significance attached to costume by the film-makers, both as a vehicle for spectacle and as a means for supporting narrative realism and cinematic illusionism. Yet, as Gaines indicates, these two impulses were contradictory: costume, in spite of the efforts to subordinate it to narrative, was frequently an eye-catching diversion from the diegesis. But if costume was supposed to defer to the demands of realism, the body – particularly the female body – was subservient to costume design. The bodies of female stars were completely reconstructed by the designers in the interests of both style and verisimilitude.

This brings us back to the idea of fetishism: costume would appear to be complicit with mainstream cinema's perceived project to fix the woman as object of male fantasy. Costume is the fetish obliterating 'true' femininity. Gaines questions this view, arguing that because costume has its own aesthetic, a sartorial language which reaches beyond cinema, and is in fact independent of the body, it is capable of frustrating voyeurism. She also suggests that fetishism, in that it is motivated by a desire to possess and collect objects and is therefore a substitute for looking, might be the finish of voyeurism itself. Fetishism, rather than simply oppressing women, can be seen as empowering the devotee to some extent:

> The waist-cinched 'sweetheart' bride, the Victorian tight-lacer, the anorexic and the romance novel reader all represent what was missed in the original notion of dominant culture: the muffled protests against oppression found in the very practices which seem to most graphically implement and spell out the patriarchal wish (Gaines and Herzog, 1990, p. 23).

Gaines also confronts the notion of masquerade as it has been developed in feminist theory, from Claire Johnston's essay on *Anne of the Indies* (Jacques Tourneur, 1951), in which it is used to elaborate the way in which the phallic woman becomes 'merely the trace of the exclusion

and repression of Woman' (Johnston, 1975, p. 24), to its later formula-
tions, which yield the possibility of trans-sex identification, and of
masquerade as exposure and critique. Some feminists have argued (for
example, Kuhn, 1985) that masquerade's function as sexual disguise
allows for spectatorial cross-dressing and the unmasking of culturally
defined gender categories. Once again, ideas of costume as essentially
oppressive have been dramatically shifted and its radical potential has
been recognised. Gaines argues that the ambiguities inherent in costume
can be exploited to disrupt traditional ways of perceiving gender
identities, and that the critic can become a kind of cross-dresser, setting
categories at odds with each other in her own play with meaning.
Although these ideas are articulated specifically with respect to sexual
identity, they also have relevance to national identity, as I shall demonstrate.

In her article on costume and narrative in the same anthology, Gaines
delves deeper into Hollywood's contradictory attitude to costume
(Gaines, 1990). On one hand, dress is seen as transmitting essential
information about character to the viewer: it is an exterior indicator of
the inner self. In this respect, it must match, or fit, the actor's role – there
must be continuity between interior and exterior. Gaines sees this idea of
costume 'matching' the self as originating in nineteenth-century notions
of identity, which recast eighteenth-century beliefs that the self was a
separate, fixed entity inaccessible to public scrutiny. Whereas in the 18th
century, display was simply an exterior phenomenon which could signify
any number of concepts, in the 19th, dress became a window to the soul,
expressing personality, social status and so on: the exterior provided
clues to the interior. From this point, Gaines suggests, dress became
more anonymous, reflecting social fears that it gave away too much.
From the earliest days of cinema, costume was seen as an extension of
acting. Stylistic flourishes were discouraged in case they disrupted the
unity of the film. This helps to explain critical neglect of screen costume
design: we are encouraged to 'see through' clothes to the inner persona,
and the impulse towards realism in cinematic dress reinforces its
invisibility.

On the other hand, cinema's investment in spectacle lends enormous
importance to costume and to costume designers, who bring their own
individual style to the movie, and feed in another layer of meaning. The
designer's identity, or signature, overlays both the star persona and the
movie character, and competes with other creative identities (director,
cinematographer, production designer and so on) for recognition. This

process has little to do with narrative or character – indeed, it diverts attention from these concerns. The spectator is distracted into a reverie detached from the film's storyline. This 'design extravagance' is distinct from, but related to, the 'textural extravagance' characteristic of costume in melodrama, where visual excess reinforces the emotional charge carried by the *mise en scène*, yet by its very artistry threatens to undermine the emotional response (Gaines, 1990, p. 205). Formal display demands an aesthetic appreciation at odds with its function in melodrama as carrier of affect. What Gaines calls 'the costume idiolect' has an existence independent of narrative spatial and temporal codes, producing aberrant messages which directors such as Hitchcock saw as ruining the subtle moments in a scene. Yet this idiolect is not completely free of the chains of narrative: rather, it appears at an obtuse angle to it.

Gaines's article goes a long way towards opening up the complex and contradictory role played by costume in cinema, and the opportunities it offers cultural critics to rethink feminist film theory's anti-Hollywood stance. By contrast, Maureen Turim's article on the New Look in the same volume adopts a more conventional feminist line (Turim, 1990). Since the New Look is relevant to the use of costume in the Gainsborough films under consideration, her arguments merit serious consideration. Turim contends, following a general consensus, that Christian Dior's New Look, launched properly in 1947, though it had been mooted before, was instrumental in re-feminising women for the post-war drive to place women back in the family. During the war, partly due to austerity programmes, female dress had been masculinised. Tailored utility clothing both matched military uniforms, enlisting everyone in the war effort, and empowered the women who wore it, endowing them with a masculine ruthlessness. The sculptured look evoked modernist abstraction, while the flowing curves of the New Look nostalgically recalled the past and, for many, outmoded ideas of femininity. It also, in its fulsome extravagance, recognised the role of women in post-war consumerism.

Dior's creation remoulded the female form. Straight lines and angles gave way to softly curved shoulders and hourglass figures nipped in by corsets, uplifted by pointed bras and padded out by crinolines. The emphasis on breasts and hips seemed to accentuate women's fertility, suggesting that their social role from now on would be reproductive rather than productive. In *June Bride* (Bretaigne Windust, 1948), Bette Davis wore her first New Look wardrobe: the story concerned a magazine editor who decides to give up her successful career for marriage. Turim traces the ideological significance of the New Look

Refashioning post-war femininity: Dior's New Look

Left: Uniform chic: *Vogue* advertisement (1943)
Right: Never mind Paris: wartime women wore dungarees for work and play

through a number of 50s movies, concluding that its symbolic power in redrawing gender boundaries resided in the way it connoted an exaggerated female sexuality. The decorative folds and ruffles in soft, luxurious fabrics, the flowers which adorned the dresses, put the eroticised female body on display after a long period during which it had been rendered invisible. For Turim, this confirms the New Look's reactionary status:

> Just as these decorative dresses were often very uncomfortable and impractical to wear, so the decorative and passive function assigned to women by their metaphorical inscription in such clothing was the ugly underside of the charming appearance. In fact, the sweetheart line [New Look] can also be seen as a form of guilded bondage (Turim, 1990, p. 227).

Elizabeth Wilson in *Adorned in Dreams* (Wilson, 1985) shares Turim's antagonism, seeing in the New Look a morbid, backward looking romanticism which she links to fascist ideology. Developed in Paris during the Nazi occupation, it has been described as a 'fashion of collaborators and Germans'. Wilson herself remarks that the style indicates a remarkable persistence in the late 40s of the romantic styles that had flowered under Nazism, in a world supposedly dedicated to the exorcising of Fascism (Wilson, 1985, p. 44). It is yet another indication of the social significance of fashion that the New Look was so controversial at the time, and continues to be so. If we look closer at the contemporary debates, some interesting assumptions about gender emerge which persist in recent feminist arguments.

In Britain, the New Look did not have an altogether easy passage into the hearts, minds and shops of the nation. It was resisted on a number of grounds (Phillips, 1963). Not least as a reason for refusal was the post-war economic crisis. Austerity measures were still in force, and Stafford Cripps, President of the Board of Trade, suggested to the British Guild of Creative Designers that they would be helping the national effort by keeping the short skirt popular in Britain. Labour Party feminists objected that because of general shortages, the longer, fuller skirts would only be available to the well-off. Some also objected to the change in body image. Mabel Ridealgh wrote in *Reynolds's News*:

> Our modern world has become used to the freedom of short, sensible clothing and prefers simplicity to over-dressiness, false padding, and

Short but not sweet: masculinised wartime fashion

exaggerated design. ... Women today are taking a larger part in the happenings of the world and the New Look is too reminiscent of a caged bird's attitude. I hope our fashion dictators will realise the new outlook of women and will give the death blow to any attempt at curtailing women's freedom (Phillips, 1963, p. 132).

Women who had experienced the war as emancipating were naturally reluctant to relinquish their new-found freedoms and power. Yet there was more to the resistance than that. First, there was the 'foreignness' of the New Look: the status of Paris as world leader in haute couture had declined during the war, and Dior's 1947 collection was a bid to regain lost ground, both economic and ideological. It is interesting in this respect that a 1949 British film, *Maytime in Mayfair*, directed by Herbert Wilcox and starring Anna Neagle and Michael Wilding, took as its subject competition between English and French fashion houses over who was responsible for designing the New Look. British distrust of the French, traditionally focused on their excessive sexuality, and exacerbated by their collaboration, surfaces in negative responses to the New Look: it was too sexy, too extravagant and phoney. Then, there was its Romantic nostalgia: at the end of the war, people were anxious to look forward rather than back, to build a new Britain. The past was full of horrors they would rather forget, and was better erased. On the other hand, in its abundance it did look forward – to the promise of a new consumerism which, in depressed 1947 Britain, seemed like a pipe dream. One gets the feeling, too, that the extreme femininity of Dior's design was threatening not only to women masculinised by the war, but to a vulnerable male population returning home, fearful of being outnumbered, swamped by a feminised culture. The New Look aroused primitive fears about female sexuality: both women and men dreaded being swallowed up by an overwhelming maternal body.

Many of these fears are present in recent feminist approaches to fashion. The female body moulded to emphasise femininity is oppressive,

Britain's New Look: Anna Neagle in *Maytime in Mayfair*

while its masculinisation – the wearing of trousers, or tailored suits – is emancipatory and connotes modernity. The former suggests that women are not like men, while the latter suggests they can be, with all the advantages that seems to imply. Yet, as Elizabeth Wilson points out, the New Look was strangely androgynous:

> The models were tall as guardsmen, and their street clothes resembled those of guardsmen in mufti, or city men leaning against furled umbrellas. They wore the highest high heels, and hobble skirts with sharply jutting hips and flying panels which bore faint memories of Gothic architecture, but the hard hats looked like city bowlers (Wilson, 1985, p. 46).

It appears that what was at stake in the New Look was the assertion of a feminine androgyny over the masculine one prevalent during the war. It also appears that the latter was more acceptable to both women and men than the former.

Marjorie Garber's book on cross-dressing, *Vested Interests* (Garber, 1992), attempts to break open the troublesome question of costume's relationship to identity by looking in detail at transvestism, both historically and in terms of the ways in which it has been explained in medical discourses. Her study hinges on a polemic about transvestism itself: rather than 'looking through' the transvestite to the 'true' gender beneath the disguise, we should see him/her in their own right – as a 'third term' which challenges binary gender categories. For Garber, the most important aspect of transvestism is the question it provokes: 'Is this a man, a woman, or both?' The category crisis generated by transvestism, argues Garber, exposes the undecidability of gender, and of meaning itself.

Vested Interests is a major work of scholarship which finally brings to the fore the fundamental social and cultural significance of costume. Most usefully for my own argument, Garber widens the discussion to include the way dress formulates sexual and national identity – the one often folded over the other. She points to the power dress has always had to define social behaviour: the medieval and Renaissance sumptuary laws, which forbade the lower classes from dressing in the same costume as their masters, is compared with the Nazi 'dress code' for Jews and homosexuals. Both were intended to enforce social hierarchies and ensure that identity could be 'read' without ambiguity or confusion. When, in response to Nazi edict, the King of Denmark donned a yellow star and urged compatriots to do the same, he mobilised precisely the category confusion which sumptuary regulations are intended to control.

Sumptuary laws in England reached a peak during the reign of Elizabeth I – Garber, a Shakespeare scholar, connects the obsession with cross-dressing and gender uncertainty in Elizabethan theatre to this fact. An extraordinary passage from the 'Homily Against Excess in Apparel', which Elizabeth commanded to be read out in the churches, states very clearly how the representative Englishman should be clothed – renouncing costly, 'foppish' apparel for 'honest and comely' dress (Garber, 1992, p. 27). Effeminacy, profligacy and sartorial excess, the whims of fashion are all to be avoided if the Englishman is to be legible as English, and lend patriotic support to the national economy. For Garber, what is important here is the way a number of social categories collide and conflict:

> Dancing shirts, ruffles, face painting – all of the Homily's iconographic indicators of excess could be dislocated from the context of sumptuary laws and rearticulated as signs of another kind of vestimentary transgression, one that violated expected boundaries of gender identification or gender decorum. For one kind of crossing, inevitably, crosses over into another: the categories of 'class' and 'rank', 'estate and condition' which seem to contain and regulate gender ('earls and above'; 'knights' wives'), are, in turn, interrogated by it. As we will see throughout this study, class, gender, sexuality, and even race and ethnicity – the determinate categories of analysis for modern and postmodern cultural critique – are themselves brought to crisis in dress codes and sumptuary regulation (Garber, 1992, p. 28).

For my own purposes, Elizabethan dress codes are remarkably similar to the sumptuary regulations in force during the Second World War. Once again, ostensibly for economic reasons, excess in apparel and make-up was banned. The utility clothing scheme provided garments which were nothing if not restrained and, as I have already noted, a masculinised tailored look, close to military uniforms, prevailed. For the purposes of national unity, sexual difference was substantially effaced: as in Elizabethan times, stable national identity was seen to reside in 'honest and comely' attire stripped of frippery and foppery – in effect, de-feminised (although, as Antonia Lant points out in *Blackout*, 1991, the government was anxious not to lose the signs of sexual difference altogether, and commissioned a special Berlei corset which could be worn under uniforms to retain 'feminine curves'). This throws light on the scandal caused by the excessive femininity of the New Look, and on the hostility which greeted the Gainsborough costume dramas with their (relatively) lavish dress and decor and their conjuring up of an erotically charged feminine world. The wartime sumptuary restrictions, and their regulation of feminine excess, fed into the debates about British national cinema, which, as we saw in the previous chapter, inveighed against Hollywood glamour in favour of ordinary characters and a restrained aesthetic of realism. Here, I want to look more closely at Garber's ideas about transvestism and category crisis.

Garber sees the transvestite as a kind of uncanny figure, a 'boundary phenomenon' of the type discussed in James Donald's account of identity instability (Donald, 1992). If the founding of sexual identity depends upon the marking of a border between male and female, and the expulsion of each from the other, the transvestite returns to haunt the frontier, is created by the very act of expulsion. For Garber, the transvestite has no 'true' sexual identity – he/she exists to mock the idea of true or stable identity itself.

Display and excess are crucial to transvestite transgression. Garber picks up the concept of fetishism, so important to feminist film theory, and argues, as do other recent commentators (for example, Studlar, 1990), that its oscillation between knowledge and disavowal, its fantasy of the detachable phallus, can be a source of empowerment for women. She also reassesses the idea of masquerade, turning it round from a mechanism to exclude and repress woman to an assertion of femininity. She quotes Lacan to the effect that: 'The fact that femininity finds its refuge in this mask, by virtue of the fact of the [repression] inherent in the phallic mark of desire, has the curious consequence of making virile display in the human being itself seem feminine ('The Signification of the Phallus', 291)' (Garber, 1992, p. 355).

Thus the phallus is haunted by what it attempts to repress, which returns to flaunt its terms and conditions. The fetish object, displayed as phallic substitute, by its very existence betrays the fact that no one has the phallus. In this account, femininity itself is a boundary phenomenon, hovering on the periphery of the masculine identity, against which everything is measured and found wanting, to remind it of its own lack. It is precisely this capacity to expose and critique that, argues Garber, lies at the heart of our unease when confronted with the transvestite's flamboyant sexual disguise.

Garber's analysis of the part played by costume in fixing and unsettling ethnic identity is equally illuminating. She traces the stigmatisation of Jews through sumptuary laws as far back as Roman times, describing how Jewish men have historically been demeaned by being labelled effeminate. She quotes a passage from *Mein Kampf* in which Adolf Hitler recollects meeting the phantom of Jewishness in the streets of Vienna:

'Once, as I was strolling through the Inner City', Hitler writes, 'I suddenly encountered an apparition in a black caftan and black hair locks. Is this a Jew? was my first thought'. And the longer he 'stared at this foreign face, scrutinising feature for feature, the more my first question assumed a new form: Is this a German?' The 'unclean dress and ... generally unheroic appearance of the Jews', 'these caftan-wearers', convince Hitler that he is face to face with otherness – with the not-self (which is to say, the self he fears) (Garber, 1992, p. 227).

I have already discussed the feminisation of the Other in the context of Orientalism with reference to Donald's analysis of *The Mystery of Dr Fu Manchu* (Donald, 1992). For Hitler, the Jew becomes the 'underground self' described by Edward Said. The Jew's uncertain gender is pivotal to Hitler's question about his ethnic origin: he is racially impure because he is sexually indeterminate.

Garber shows how sexual and racial ambivalence can be eroticised – as with the character of the Sheik personified by Rudolf Valentino, who was himself the butt of American xenophobia directed at his effeminacy (Garber, 1992, p. 361). She also examines Lord Byron's notorious Orientalism, seeing in Don Juan's obsession with cross-dressing a potential exposure of the very mechanisms of Orientalism:

By locating transvestism, strategically, in an Eastern locale, Byron deploys the chic of Araby, its sexual and sartorial destabilisations, as a powerful fantasy as well as a social critique. The poem dramatises transvestic disguise both as involuntary transformation and as wish fulfilment, while preserving – because of its 'Oriental' setting – the escape hatch of the dream. Like the cross-dressed Juan – and the cross-dressed Duchess – his supporting cast of eunuchs, fops and epicenes personify the very real power of transvestism not as a carnivalised stage elsewhere, an exotic other, but rather as a reminder of the repressed that always returns (Garber, 1992, p. 321).

The transvestite brings it all back home, reminding us that the place where we hope to feel secure can never be stable. The foundations of identity are constantly shifting. In her discussion of cross-dressing and impersonation, Garber refers to the Elvis Presley imitators who sprang up after his death. According to Presley's biographer Albert Goldman, some of them underwent plastic surgery in order to become indistinguishable from their idol, transforming themselves into effigies. As Garber points out:

> We are very close here to Freud's notion of the uncanny repetition-compulsion, the *heimlich* transformed into the *unheimlich*, castration anxiety, the multiplication of doubles, 'something repressed which recurs'. Meantime at Graceland, the Presley home (*Heim?*) and museum in Memphis, his costumes live, too, on mannequins ... for the delectation of the faithful. Elvis as ghost comes home to rejoin the ghostly twin brother whose grave has been moved to the Graceland memorial garden (Garber, 1992, p. 371).

Elvis's doubles, and his preserved costumes, are rather like the living dead stalking the graveyard of identity. They suggest, as all costume does, that the past is always in the present, however much we would prefer to leave it behind. Cross-dressing is as much a manifestation of a wish to be somewhere else – in another time or place – as someone else. This brings us back to the notion of vagrant identities. The cross-dresser is a kind of traveller, never at home in his/her suit of clothes. We are not talking here of simple binary oscillations – between male/female, East/West, inside/outside, here/there, for instance – but of a complex mapping of fluctuation between categories across one another. Once identity is viewed in this light as a hybrid state, then the way is open to transforming national identity.

IV

THE LURE OF THE PAST:
REINVENTING HISTORY

Between 1943 and 1950, the British studio Gainsborough produced a cycle of costume dramas that provoked a cultural scandal equal to – if not greater than – that caused by some of the Powell and Pressburger films. The hostility of many of the British quality press to Powell and Pressburger has been well documented, notably by Ian Christie in his analysis of contemporary responses to *Peeping Tom* (Michael Powell, 1959). Christie attributes the critics' disgust (more than one of them describes the film as effluence which should be flushed away) to a characteristic antipathy towards the transgressive pleasures of cinema itself, which reach beyond the strictures of good taste and respectability to our most disorderly impulses (Christie, 1978). This defence amounts to a High Romantic argument against a certain (bourgeois) tendency in British culture to impose a utilitarian aesthetic devoted to liberal humanist concerns. And, indeed, it has been in such terms – the flaunting of cinematic specificity and the flouting of criteria of quality – that Powell and Pressburger have since been rehabilitated as great British film-makers.

On the face of it, the case for the Gainsborough costume dramas is similar: their fanciful narratives, flamboyantly decorative *mise en scène*, and irreverent disregard for verisimilitude proved distinctly indigestible to critics dedicated to supporting a national cinema defined in terms of authenticity and aesthetic restraint. Thus Simon Harcourt-Smith, writing in *Tribune* in response to *The Wicked Lady* (Leslie Arliss, 1945), could scarcely stomach it:

> Perhaps because I am, by inclination at least, an historian, *The Wicked Lady* arouses in me a nausea out of proportion to the subject. Perhaps I should not cavil at this complete misunderstanding of Restoration

De-bunking history: Margaret Lockwood and James Mason in *The Wicked Lady*

England, the tatty Merry English Roadhouse atmosphere, with the bowls of 'daffies' on the gate-legged tables, and the ladylike carousings of pretty Miss Margaret Lockwood, with a James Mason so embarrassed and yet so competent as the highwayman, that he aroused at once both admiration and sympathy. ... The tedium, the grey ruin of modern life have obviously turned the costume picture into, perhaps, the most promising film gamble of today. ... By all means let us escape on the wings of the movies to less troubled epochs than the present. What more sumptuous, sexy and witty age could you find than the Restoration? But for the Lord's sake let's evoke it properly, let's use authentic material, the life of Pepys or of Charles II himself. ... In short, if the future of the British film industry hangs, as some say, on the success of *The Wicked Lady*, then let us dispense with that future (quoted in Aspinall and Murphy, 1983, p. 74).

Madonna of the Seven Moons (Arthur Crabtree, 1944) received an equally queasy response from Helen Fletcher in *Time and Tide*:

If *Love Story* charmed you, the chances are *Madonna of the Seven Moons* will too. If *Love Story* evoked in you, as it did in me, a sort of nausea, well, here is nausea back again. ... Whether this film is being religious or sensual it remains the purplest production English cinema has yet achieved. It's the sort of dream dreamed in the last century by a lonely governess sipping her cocoa over *Jane Eyre*. See it anyway to delight your sense of the ridiculous and to feast your eyes on some of the ugliest and most expensive sets ever contrived (Fletcher, 1944).

Leaving aside, for the moment, the feminophobia close to the surface in both these reviews, the writers' uncontrollable bodily reaction seems excessive, to say the least. Their nausea implies that the films churn up something unwelcome within them which must be expelled. I shall argue that it was an unpalatable combination of femininity, foreignness and lack of authenticity which made so many of the quality critics gag. For now, I want to stay with the Powell and Pressburger comparison in order to explore why the Gainsborough costume dramas, though they are consistently linked to the Powell and Pressburger films in revisionist histories of British cinema (for example, Barr, 1986), have not been rehabilitated in British film culture to the same extent.

In his defence of Michael Powell in 'The Scandal of *Peeping Tom*', Ian Christie is careful not to reposition the director within a 'high art' canon, asserting that the value of his work lies in the way it 'operates precisely in the space between "good" and "bad" taste' (Christie, 1978, p. 59). Powell is 'the principle of cinematic specificity at work in British cinema', an assertion backed up with a footnote in which Powell himself, interviewed by two French critics in 1968, claims: 'I'm not a director with a personal style, I am simply cinema' (Christie, 1978, p. 59). In one fell swoop, Christie confirms Powell's renegade status in British culture while conferring authority on him via a claim to 'pure cinema' – beyond all canons, outside genre, gender and nationality. The tables are neatly turned, transforming Powell from agent of pollution into *agent provocateur*.

No such claims to purity can be made to legitimate the 40s Gainsborough costume dramas. They are blatantly genre pieces and genre is notoriously mixed. There is no identifiable directorial voice to enable them to transcend their lowly status, as was argued for those Hollywood melodramas directed by Douglas Sirk, say, or Vincente Minnelli (Elsaesser, 1987; Nowell-Smith, 1987; Mulvey, 1987). Their re-entry into British film culture in the early 80s came about as a result of the reassessment of British cinema on one hand, and renewed feminist interest in melodrama and the women's picture on the other (Aspinall and Murphy, 1983). And that, it would seem, was that. In spite of being linked with the anti-consensual themes of Powell and Pressburger, the Gainsborough melodramas have consistently been ignored or marginalised in debates about national identity in 40s British cinema – either subsumed into the consensus (Richards, 1988), left out of discussion altogether (Hurd, 1984), or pushed to the edges of arguments about the critically sanctioned films (Lant, 1991; Higson, 1995). Sue Harper's work stands almost alone in asserting the central relevance of Gainsborough to revisionist histories of British cinema. Some of the reasons for this neglect have been suggested in Chapter II. Here, I want to look more closely at the particular conjunction of factors which render the short-lived cycle of Gainsborough costume dramas so troublesome, not only for critics at the time of their release, but also for more recent commentators. This will require a detour through the embattled territory of the historical film.

The historical film re-presents the past for the purposes of the present and the future. The status of this process of reworking history is always open to question, to a greater or lesser degree depending upon the perceived accuracy – authenticity – of its depictions. One of the problems is the broad range of movies that qualify as historical films: westerns, biopics, period romances and musicals, biblical epics, almost anything that takes 'history' as its subject matter and dresses it up in period clothes and decor. Within this wide spectrum, films which pay attention to verisimilitude are usually given greater value, in critical terms at least, than those which take liberties with history. Yet the obsession with period authenticity reveals a contradiction at the heart of the historical film: the symbolic carriers of period detail – costume, hair, decor – are notoriously slippery and anachronistic. They are intertextual sign systems with their own logic which constantly threatens to disrupt the concerns of narrative and dialogue. Costume historian Anne Hollander has suggested a tension in historical films between surface verisimilitude, in which costume signals are used to give a broadly correct sense of period, and a more playful use of historically inaccurate detail which can transmit contemporary information about beauty and fashion (Hollander, 1974).

This tension between truthfulness and infidelity, and the heterogeneity characteristic of the historical film's encounters with the past, are a constant irritation for critics and official agencies concerned with the role of history in national culture – though audiences are evidently well able to accommodate historical licence. Clearly, what is at stake is the status of history itself as truth, a vital issue when it comes to representing the national past. The contradictory nature of the historical film, the tendency of costume and period display to appear as masquerade, brings it uncomfortably close to presenting history as fabrication.

Sue Harper has traced this anxiety surrounding the historical film through official efforts in 30s and 40s Britain to manage and control the representation of history in feature films (Harper, 1994). Bodies such as the Historical Association put the question of national history firmly on the agenda, couching their arguments in terms of the necessity for accuracy and truth in the representation of Britain's past. Harper shows how some producers, swayed by such arguments and also influenced by the drive for a national quality cinema, took steps to legitimate their productions by employing period advisers — a kind of quality control mechanism. Others, however, flouted the official strictures, recognising that popular audiences cared little for verisimilitude. Indeed, the audiences' pleasure in historical films was intimately bound up with their sense of play and licence. The 30s Alexander Korda period spectaculars and the wartime Gainsborough costume dramas were among those that delighted audiences while displeasing critics, and Harper's work feeds interestingly into Antonia Lant's arguments about the impetus towards realism and restraint in wartime consensus movies (Lant, 1991). Such tussles over authenticity in historical film clearly have a long genealogy, and certain arguments and attitudes towards history persist in recent debates too.

Nigel Mace, writing about historical epics in wartime British cinema (Mace, 1988), cites Pierre Sorlin's thesis in *The Film in History* (Sorlin, 1980) to the effect that historical films are worthy objects for study because they reveal the process whereby the present is reorganised using the pretext of the past, and because they represent one of the ways in which ideas of the past are created at specific moments and become part of a general cultural historiography. The attraction of this contention for the social historian is not difficult to grasp: the historical film both reflects prevailing social conditions and contributes to current ideas about history — both can be directly read from the films' narrative themes. Mace proceeds to analyse four wartime costume films for the ways in which they reflect audiences' contemporary sense of the crisis through which they were passing, and official views of the present and future of Britain. The result is a static, fossilised view of history as a coherent set of ideas straightforwardly accessible in the films themselves.

What is more, Mace's concern with finding films which conform to his criteria of re-presenting a contemporary Churchillian discourse in the guise of Britain's national past, as with other contributions to the debates around national identity in wartime British cinema, limits him to an unacceptably narrow range of films. In his desire to extract truths about the present from representations of the past, he by-passes the very elements, so crucial to the genre, that would problematise the search for truth in itself: costume and decor, the agents of duplicity.

The educative approach to historical film surfaces in recent, more sophisticated accounts. Writing about the 80s cycle of British 'heritage' movies, Andrew Higson, while paying attention to visual codes and the films' delight in spectacle, is distrustful of their tendency to pastiche (Higson, 1993a). For Higson, the 80s heritage films put the past on display, petrifying a heritage culture and presenting it as an attractively packaged consumer item. He identifies a tension between this self-conscious visual splendour and the levels of ironic critique of Britain's imperial and colonialist past offered by the narrative and dialogue, often traceable to the source novels. It is interesting that this very tension between script and visual codes is used by Sue Harper (1983; 1994) in precisely the reverse manner to validate the popular appeal of the Gainsborough costume films.

For Higson, the nostalgic gaze at a visually splendid reconstruction of conservative, pastoral Englishness gets in the way of what he sees as a more authentic view of Britain's past: the loss of empire, the decline of British liberalism, the crumbling of national inheritance. This narrative of loss is offset and undermined by images of visual plenitude which stress stability rather than change. Higson's argument represents an impressive elaboration of the 80s left critique of what was perceived as the Thatcherite heritage industry (see also Corner and Harvey, 1991) and is clearly part of a specific project. Nevertheless, his analysis manifests many of the symptoms evident in critical approaches to the historical film: a distrust of decoration and display, which is perceived as obfuscating a more genuinely authentic approach to history; a fear of being 'swallowed up' by nostalgia and a concomitant desire for critical distance and irony; a view of history as necessarily offering lessons for the present; and a sense that history should somehow remain uncontaminated by commodification (Higson's *Waving the Flag*, 1995, puts forward a more extended critique of the heritage film's use of spectacle and pictorialism to commodify and fetishise the past). Many of these ideas find an echo in earlier approaches. Particularly pervasive is the desire to recover some kind of inner truth from behind the trappings of historical reconstruction. With such instrumentalist criteria in play, it is hardly surprising that the Gainsborough costume dramas with their irreverent treatment of history and naked lack of authenticity should be almost as unacceptable now as in the 40s.

At the risk of digressing too far from the subject at hand, it is worth looking more closely at Freud's article on the uncanny for clues as to why our encounters with the past inspire such defensive reactions. These encounters appear to involve the dangers of loss of identity already reflected in the preceding chapters on national identity and costume. Freud's notion of the uncanny (Freud, 1990) hinges on a relationship between past and present. At the centre of this enigmatic, richly evocative essay lies the idea of the compulsion to repeat, whereby we are driven to replay and revisit past occurrences. What starts out as amusing coincidence soon becomes alarming as our compulsive return to familiar territory takes on the hue of a trap from which we may never escape (as Freud points out, the familiar/*heimlich* is inextricably bound up with the uncanny/*unheimlich*). History, or past events, are overshadowed by our fear that we may never be able to extricate ourselves from them in order to move forward. (In a conversation with film historian Linda Williams, she described herself to me as having allowed herself to become 'lost in the archive' in relation to one of her projects – a phrase which precisely sums up the pleasures and perils of historical research.) To put history in its place, at a distance, renders it 'safe', or *heimlich*, once more. It is illuminating that Freud's example of the compulsion to repeat is based on one of his own experiences, in which he was unable to find his way out of the red light district in a foreign city. The *unheimlich* is thus specifically associated with 'aberrant' female sexuality, which is desired as well as feared.

Closely linked to the compulsion to repeat is the sense we have of being under a spell, which Freud attributes to the resurfacing of 'primitive' modes of thought, which are assumed to have been overcome, and whose recurrence takes on magical, or uncanny, significance. This idea clearly undermines any notion of history as a series of progressions from 'savage' to 'civilised' values, since both these terms co-exist in the present for Freud. The past thus becomes a threat to the present; or, more precisely, primitive emotions consigned to the past threaten to erupt into the present and disturb our civilised, rational thoughts. It is not difficult to find an echo of this concept in the rejection of nostalgia – symptomatic of a desire to ward off the past – so central to left writing on national identity. And it is there in the distrust of imaginary plenitude believed to characterise history as spectacle, and the recourse to a critical, reasoned view of history. In the Freudian scenarios, such defensive action is bound to fail, since our present psychic existence is forever haunted by past thoughts and feelings: the return of the repressed.

Freud underplays the uncertainty at the heart of uncanny experiences – a doubt about whether we are in the realms of the real or of simulacra. It is just such uncertainty that much historical writing strives to overcome, by establishing the truth of the past and separating it definitively from the present. Yet it can never entirely surmount the chaotic amalgam of past and present that is history, as the phenomenon of the double testifies. The impulse behind the Egyptian custom of creating effigies of the dead in an attempt to ward off extinction resonates with other attempts to preserve the past in portraits, statues and, indeed, in bio-pics of famous people long dead. These modern-day effigies could be said to bear an uncanny resemblance to, rather than provide a truthful replica of, their subjects. They suggest the uncertainty, the undecidability of the relationship between the dead and the living. What begins as an attempt to seek comfort against the inevitability of death, ends up as a reminder that the living are always haunted by the dead.

Freud's short essay is very suggestive for my own argument about approaches to historical film. The desire to authenticate historical film, to seek its truth, seems to be founded on a need to establish it as real rather than fantastic, or as somewhere between the two. Official historians, and even recent commentators on official histories, find it difficult to accept a notion of history as oscillating between reality and fantasy. Feminist cultural historians, it seems, are often less wary of travesties of the past, perhaps because official histories have generally served them ill.

Alison Light sees the historical novels she read in childhood as unofficial, popular histories at odds with the culturally sanctioned literature taught at school (Light, 1989). Although they do have an educative function, their relationship to the past is primarily one of fantasy: they offer possibilities of adventure and self-fulfilment for women outside home, family and nation. Where the realist novel may question women's traditional roles, in the end it resolves matters in a 'that's how it is' manner. For Light, historical novels open up the past to wayward subjectivities – though she is ambivalent about their focus on extraordinary women:

The transposition into a historical past is necessarily double-edged. On the one hand, contemporary mores can be differently placed and

71

explored: these heroines are able to take up what would usually be seen as the masculine reins of power and sexual autonomy; on the other hand, precisely because they are not 'ordinary' women, and this is not realism, such figures are self-proclaimed as 'escapist': as romantic fantasies, they are compensating registers of profound discontent, whilst remaining mediated and distorted expressions of it. ... It is typical, however, that the historical transformation of the contemporary feminine choices is imagined upwards (as it were) into the aristocratic or royal setting – these are rags-to-riches novels in many cases. The expansive and dynamic existences of a Young Bess or a Mary Stuart are a magical compromise with the anguish of a feminine subjectivity; they cannot literally be contemporary models, which is at once their attraction and their fault (Light, 1989, p. 66).

Turning to the novels' representation of Englishness, Light identifies a backward-looking, conservative vision of the nation state as unified, which goes against the grain of their emancipatory vision of femininity, and which she finds much harder to take, even though she acknowledges its part in forming her own subjectivity. Ultimately, however, there is something more than political correctness at stake:

The study of popular fictions will always founder on the rock of ideological purity, clung to in political desperation. Not least because the identifications which all literary texts offer are multiple and conflictual, even irreconcilable. The problem with all novels is always the one thing which is pleasurable about them: their fictitiousness. Though they give us a semblance of reality, they draw too upon feelings, upon unspoken assumptions and unknown desires. Ultimately no one can legislate for when we wander the twilight world of reading, laying down in advance what we might wish to encounter, and which bits we'll simply ignore. What's clear is that the capacity to fantasise which novels encourage is notoriously unbiddable, and that for those of us who judge novels by their messages, moral, social or political, this has always been a mixed blessing (Light, 1989, p. 69).

In spite of her ambivalence, Light offers a much more open and dynamic account of the uses of the past in popular fiction than is to be found in the approaches considered above. Many of her insights are relevant to my own arguments: the validation of what is usually dismissed as 'escapist' fare by emphasising the positive role of fantasy in conjuring up the past; a celebration of the reading process as a kind of wandering through texts which enables us to pick up and discard identities at will (it is interesting that Higson, 1993a, p. 112, is more disparaging about such tourism in relation to the heritage film); and a conception of the past as a place where contemporary dilemmas are worked through, identities are tested and not necessarily resolved in a traditional manner. For Light, the past in historical fictions is sexier than the present, and she is hesitant about such nostalgia. But I would argue that the past in such fictions is never simply the past: they look backwards and forwards at the same time, creating a heterogeneous world that we enter and leave like travellers, in a constant movement of exile and return.

In *Forever England*, Light discusses Daphne Du Maurier's romance with the past, seeing in her heroines' identification with swashbuckling male adventurers a desire to be differently female (Light, 1991). Du Maurier reorders the boundaries of sexual difference by putting at the centre of her historical romances a feminine desire to escape the constrictions of 'home' equal to that of male literary figures such as Paul Fussell, D. H. Lawrence or Louis MacNeice with their bitter hatred of a domesticated, suburbanised England. Indeed, Du Maurier's heroines are often escapologists, extricating themselves from tight corners – or from tight clothing – which provide metaphors for the bondage of feminine existence. Such mental and physical cross-dressing carries with it danger as well as pleasure. In transgressing sexual and national boundaries, Du Maurier's heroines run the risk of death or permanent exile. Though they always return home in the end, it is with a sense of regret – shared by the reader – for what has been lost in the retreat to safety.

In Du Maurier's fiction, the past is rarely simply a 'safe place' whose forbidden subjects may be harmlessly rehearsed. It haunts the present, unsettling stable identities and destroying the very notion of home as a haven, or place of rest. We are close here to Freud's compulsion to repeat, the uncanny relationship between past and present, in which the past is always with us in the form of doubles, effigies, in which we both lose and find ourselves. This losing and finding of identity is crucial to the pleasures of reading fiction; in historical novels or films the process is intensified by the time-travel required of readers and spectators. The well-known saying 'The past is a foreign country – they do things differently there', encapsulates the sense of loss of familiar landmarks and of becoming a stranger to oneself that historical fiction produces in the reader.

In an article on the representation of women in wartime British cinema, Sue Harper offers a similarly open account of the function of the past in historical film (Harper, 1988). She sees history in such movies as a form of narrative disguise which makes possible all kinds of unlicensed behaviour, including the interrogation of traditional gender roles. The emancipation of women into male dominated areas during the war years was no easy process, argues Harper, and women continued to be constrained both by the resistance of their male counterparts and government efforts to regulate and control the 'mobile women' who were both necessary, and a potential threat to the national interest. Yet the reality of women's wartime experiences were rarely dealt with directly in the realist home-front movies. In historical romances such as the Gainsborough costume dramas, according to Harper targeted primarily at working-class female audiences, female desire took centre stage. The spectacle of libidinous women acting in their own interests rather than those of home and country proved compelling to audiences – even if a token element of self-sacrifice was introduced by the scriptwriters as a reminder of where duty lay.

Like Light, Harper sees the function of the past in historical fiction as primarily cathartic, allowing for the working through of present day difficulties and discontents. While Harper characterises these difficulties mainly in terms of sexuality, it is significant that she draws attention to the centrality of gypsies and itineracy to the costume dramas. For Light, the 'gypsy spirit' abroad in Du Maurier's historical adventurers is a symptom of the wish to escape the suffocating confines of home, family and Englishness. Her itinerant heroines return home sadder and wiser, more aware of their need for stability and of the unlikelihood of that need being satisfied. By contrast, Harper sees the gypsy theme in 40s historical novels and films as another form of disguise, allowing for the recognition and demystification of marginal groups perceived as potential threats to society. Harper's emphasis on the domestication of marginal figures who have little or no stake in 'normal' society is suggestive, particularly in relation to the film *Jassy* (Bernard Knowles, 1947), for example, where the gypsy heroine, played by Margaret Lockwood, makes her way up the social ladder to become mistress of a splendid English mansion. Yet there is more to the gypsies in the Gainsborough costume dramas than this. While clearly functioning as metaphors for exotic 'otherness', as signifiers of ethnic impurity they are often given a central and positive role in English society, with interesting consequences for the films' portrayal of national identity.

My trip around some critical approaches to the historical film has led me as far away from the educative, instructional conception of history as it is possible to get. The historical romances considered by Light and Harper have little or no interest in period authenticity. Indeed, despite the film-makers' claims to accuracy in their promotional material, the Gainsborough costume dramas were clearly more concerned with presenting history as masquerade. One reason for the marginalisation of the Gainsborough costume dramas in discussion of national identity in British cinema seems to be an underlying desire among critics to find a more authentic version of national identity in class and gender terms than that offered by officially sanctioned discourses. Gainsborough costume romances do not lend themselves to such a project. Rather, they throw into question the very idea of authentic identities. In my view, this cavalier attitude places the costume dramas right at the heart of the issue of national identity.

As already indicated, costume plays a crucial role in the duplicity of the historical film. Even at the top end of the scale, in literary adaptations of bio-pics of great men (occasionally, women), where history is treated relatively seriously, costume has to reflect contemporary fashion as well as suggest period. In fact, the situation is generally even more complicated, since aesthetic concerns often demand considerable period slippage. In a book on Sternberg's use of costume in the films he made with Marlene Dietrich, Sybil DelGaudio analyses the flexible approach to costume and decor adopted by this notoriously extravagant director in *The Scarlet Empress* (Sternberg, 1934). Here, Marlene Dietrich as Catherine the Great was dressed in a highly stylised manner which owed more to aesthetic licence than period verisimilitude (DelGaudio, 1993). Sternberg justified his departures from historical truth in terms of artistic freedom: film was a creative medium whose task was to evoke, rather than replicate Catherine's Russia.

Significantly, the critics of the day did not agree. Sternberg's film was contrasted negatively with Alexander Korda's British bio-pic, *Catherine the Great* (Paul Czinner, 1934), which had been released shortly before and was praised for its aesthetic restraint and fidelity to history. (These claims remain to be verified – certainly Korda's film glossed over the Empress's reputed sexual excesses.) According to DelGaudio, those who hitherto had admired Sternberg's stylistic flourishes found them unacceptable in the context of a historical film, and the director's reputation never recovered. This is an indication of the vice-like grip the notion of authenticity has on the historical film. Some deviation may be tolerated, but it must not be allowed to go too far. It is also an intimation of the potential unruliness of costume.

At the bottom end of the scale, where the more disreputable costume romances belong, one would imagine more leeway might be granted. These films rarely deal with lofty subjects or the more epic aspects of history, and if they do feature the lives of famous people, it is generally from the perspective of gossip about their amorous escapades. (The Gainsborough film about Paganini, *The Magic Bow*, Bernard Knowles, 1946, and *The Bad Lord Byron*, David MacDonald, 1949, are good examples. Both use 'history' as a mere backcloth for fairly mild dramatisations of their subjects' sex lives.) Costume romances mobilise history as a site of sexual fantasy rather than a record of great deeds or celebration of national heritage. As I have already argued, fantasy depends upon multiple identifications and the transgression of boundaries of gender, class and nation, an idea well understood by those who make costume romances and by audiences, who not only accept such films' free play with period but positively relish it, if box-office success is anything to go by.

Historical infidelity: Marlene Dietrich in *The Scarlet Empress*

Historical credibility: *Catherine the Great*

Yet these historical travesties induce such symptoms of panic in critics, that it suggests there is something at stake here. Crucially, apart from their foregrounding of history as masquerade, what the costume roman-ces appear to achieve is the feminisation of history itself. This is evident in the focus on female desire as a motivating force in events, in the privileging of intimate and domestic settings and in the emphasis on fashion, hairstyles and interior decoration which are an essential factor in the films' audience appeal. And it is also there in the visual codes of costume and decor, whose decorative excess creates a feminised world in which spectacular display predominates, captivating the eye and luring it away from the concerns of narrative and dialogue. I do not need to labour the point that such feminisation, perceived as trivialisation, is offensive to those who hold to a conception of history as truth – particularly when it comes to the truth of national heritage.

Sue Harper, in an article about art direction and costume design in 40s Gainsborough costume dramas, makes some pertinent observations about their historical misdemeanours (Harper, 1983). In common with other feminist historians (see also Light, 1989; 1991), Harper character-

77

ises the costume romance as downplaying authenticity in favour of both spectacle and a focus on the intimate emotional lives of its characters. The favoured aesthetic of the Gainsborough art directors – many of whom came from non-naturalistic theatrical traditions – was 'expressionism', influenced by Reinhardt and Appia. Tim Bergfelder has questioned the critical tendency to homogenise the German influence on British production design under the label 'expressionist', and to oppose this design aesthetic too simplistically to 'realism' (Bergfelder, 1996). Nevertheless, Harper's contention that British art direction of the period owed a great deal to the influence of Europeans such as Vincent Korda, Alfred Junge and Ferdie Bellan, all of whom employed a highly decorative visual style, stands.

During the war, personnel shortages encouraged the recruitment of European creative technicians who brought with them an interest in the rococo, which went against the grain of wartime British concerns with restrained realism. But British art directors at Gainsborough such as John Bryan and Maurice Carter were also against the particular kind of understated realism preferred by other studios such as Ealing, and fostered an aesthetic which flouted historical accuracy in favour of heterogeneity. Through playful use of anachronisms, the past was explicitly created as a chaotic amalgam of conflicting styles and influences – entirely appropriate, of course, to the films' privileging of fantasy and desire. Such disregard for authenticity, together with the espousal of a feminised, decorative aesthetic, helped to put the Gainsborough costume dramas beyond the critical pale.

Costume design was equally transgressive. Elizabeth Haffenden, a key Gainsborough designer, had also worked in 30s British theatre, where some of her designs had been criticised for their expressionism. Harper claims that for the costume drama cycle, Haffenden created a kind of female genital symbolism in the women's clothes, manifest in the overt display of labial folds and pleats echoed in 'vortex' hairstyles. The scandal provoked by such extreme displays of femininity was no doubt intensified in the context of the masculinisation of female dress during the war years. Some of Haffenden's designs for the costume cycle were promoted by the studio as precursors of Dior's New Look, which outraged many in post-war Britain because of its extravagance and aggressive femininity.

Harper identifies an independent 'costume narrative' in films such as *The Wicked Lady*. Here, design works against the rather moralistic trajectory of the scripts, in which sexually aggressive women tend to come to a sticky end, by celebrating a feminine pleasure principle.

Audiences were more likely to be fired by the sexual symbolism of the costumes than to sit in judgment on the wayward women who wore them. We are back here with the disruptive potential of costume – always, it seems, a troublemaker. Harper's argument has implications for the costume dramas' representation of history. Transgressive female desire is not laid to rest in the past, as the scripts would have it. The 'costume narrative' projects a world in which the feminine principle is in the ascendancy. The significance of this for post-war redefinitions of femininity is momentous. This highly sexualised image is not exactly compatible with either wartime masculinised women or post-war projections of good motherhood.

Costume designers and art directors at Gainsborough during the 40s seem to have been given considerable creative freedom, within certain economic constraints, and were encouraged to take liberties with period authenticity, which could be expensive (Harper, 1983). Clearly, wartime economic and practical shortages exerted pressure and were substantially responsible for choices which produced the aesthetic described above. Yet the reasons so many artists dedicated to European-influenced styles found a congenial home at Gainsborough during this period have something to do with the history of the studio itself. By the 40s, Gainsborough had been a successful enterprise for twenty years or so, negotiating, through a combination of shrewd production strategies and adventurous internationalist policies, the ups and downs experienced by the British film industry during the 20s and 30s.

This is not the place for a detailed account of these events. Suffice it to say that Gainsborough had from its inception looked towards Europe for aesthetic inspiration and technical expertise, while maintaining links with Hollywood by importing American stars. This resulted in a studio style that ventured beyond the confines of a British cinema that was narrowly defined in terms of national specificity, a style that consciously projected itself as a hybrid of the national and the international. Such hybridity went against the grain of the wartime consensus – but it has also evidently proved troublesome to many subsequent cinema historians. It is Gainsborough's vagrant identity, its crossing of boundaries of nation, class and gender, that merit a central place in discussion of national identity in British cinema.

V

EUROPEAN ADVENTURES: GAINSBOROUGH STUDIOS

From the moment of its foundation by Michael Balcon and Graham Cutts in 1924, Gainsborough projected itself as an international venture. In order to break the USA's stranglehold on the British and other European markets, Balcon initiated an ambitious programme of European co-productions, while at the same time keeping an eye on the American market by borrowing Hollywood stars. Alfred Hitchcock's *The Pleasure Garden* (1925), a joint production with the Emelka Studio in Munich, was one of Balcon's first 'international' productions, heralding the German influence on Gainsborough's output in the years that followed (Seaton and Martin, 1982). Though less obviously indebted to German Expressionism than Hitchcock's *The Lodger* (1926), *The Pleasure Garden* nevertheless adopted elements of an expressionistic visual style and featured an American star, Virginia Valli. As with other Gainsborough productions, it was set in predominantly European locales, inaugurating what Seaton and Martin describe as a 'long-standing and at times obsessional involvement with life across the Channel' (Seaton and Martin, 1982a, p. 10). It seems extraordinary that Balcon, who is now almost exclusively identified with the restrained realism and 'Englishness' of Ealing, should have pursued such an aggressively internationalist policy early in his career – signs of an identity crisis here?

Seaton and Martin claim that Balcon chose the name Gainsborough as a symbol of art and quality (Seaton and Martin, 1982a, p. 11). But the association can be seen to carry more complex connotations. It is perhaps not too fanciful to delve into art history to identify more precisely what this eighteenth-century artist represents in the context of British culture and, most importantly, abroad. Despite being associated with the English School of portrait painters, which was institutionalised by Joshua Reynolds, the first president of the Royal Academy, Gainsborough's

Expressionist influence: *The Cabinet of Dr Caligari* (1919)

concerns were rather different from Reynolds's. The latter took his cue from the great Italian painters, developing the somewhat portentous genre of history paintings, in which his aristocratic sitters were depicted in classical settings, a strategy intended to add prestige to the despised portrait genre. Gainsborough, on the other hand, was influenced by eighteenth-century French painting and is considered to be the only British painter whose style is distinctively rococo. As opposed to the rather heavy realism espoused by Reynolds and other contemporaries, Gainsborough's paintings are intimate and playful, often displaying a sexual and emotional subtext and suggesting a fantasy element which extends beyond the task of achieving an accurate likeness of his sitters.

Gainsborough's portraits, with their subjects often set against lush and dramatic English landscapes, are clearly also characteristically British, apparently celebrating a serene and stable aristocratic culture and also, by including musicians, writers and actors, emphasising the creativity of the British art scene. This blend of distinctively British subject matter with a European style associated with sexuality and passion could well have been a factor in Balcon's choice of name; another may have been Gainsborough's interest in formal experiment. His use of paint was adventurous, creating the famous lustre effect on the fabric of his sitters' clothes, and he went in for high-contrast chiaroscuro patterns of light

Cesare lives: Ivor Novello in *The Lodger*

Sign of quality: the Gainsborough logo

which heightened emotional affect (shades here of the 'expressionism' so important to the Gainsborough studio aesthetic). He also experimented with optical effects, painting small landscapes on glass designed to be mounted in a box and lit from behind by a candle. Many of his paintings were left unfinished, with parts sketched in roughly, and this, together with his unique 'hatching' brushwork, drew attention to the painting process itself, thus dispensing with realism.

Without reading too much into all this, it is possible to argue that the image of 'Britishness' that Balcon wanted for Gainsborough Studios was not simply one of quality and prestige, although certainly this was an important component. The studio logo – based on Gainsborough's portrait of the actress Sarah Siddons – endured, despite several changes of management over the years. It evoked a Europeanised artistic tradition in which formal adventurousness and experiment were combined with cultural prestige and, above all, visual pleasure. There is also a sexual undercurrent suggested by the choice of Sarah Siddons's portrait: the logo celebrates a great female actress while simultaneously conjuring up the slightly risqué ambience of eighteenth-century theatre. All this is pertinent to the costume dramas considered here.

The 'British' identity that Balcon conceived for Gainsborough was a hybrid, looking to Europe for visual style and subject matter, while keeping the other eye on the USA. Indeed, Tim Bergfelder has argued that while Gainsborough took its visual aesthetics from Europe, it borrowed its narrative structure from Hollywood (Bergfelder, 1996). This kind of internationalist approach to British cinema is generally derided or ignored in debates about national identity, which tend to define Britishness in essentialist, parochial terms. Yet it is an approach which has consistently proved successful at the box-office, suggesting once again that popular taste and ideas of what constitutes Britishness are at odds with those of quality critics and official agencies. It also raises important questions about the relationship between the 'national' and the 'international' in defining national cinemas.

Andrew Higson has outlined the background to the internationalist policies of 20s and 30s British cinema, describing their base in protectionist moves to strengthen British production and distribution against American domination of world markets (Higson, 1993b). One such proposed strategy was the formation of a pan-European cartel in which the combined forces of European production, distribution and exhibition would compete directly with Hollywood on its own terms. This meant producing comparable international films: that is, films with internationally recognisable stars, high production values, American story sense and continuity standards, and a combination of American and German visual style (Germany was second only to the USA as a strong production base and market). Higson defines two tendencies in British cinema of this period: a nationalising tendency (a bid to construct a specifically national cinema), and an internationalising tendency. Clearly, both tendencies are always present – certainly they can be found in British cinema of the 40s – and always in conflict to some extent, since the international film may appear to have only a tenuous connection to national culture. Yet an indigenous national cinema must depend on international markets to survive. National cinema is also international cinema, and vice versa; we are back once more in the realms of multiple, split identities.

In the late 20s and early 30s, British film-makers such as Michael Balcon formed co-production alliances with German studios and also imported German and other central European film technicians to work in Britain. Seaton and Martin quote Gainsborough art director Maurice Carter to the effect that British art direction of the period was overwhelmingly influenced by German style – particularly that of Ufa:

> Everything we had came from Middle Europe. We looked to Berlin for technique. … Berlin was sophisticated, so we recruited German technicians and special effects experts. One of them – Alfred Jurer [sic – should be Junge] – was the mainspring and virtually ran the studio. His contract gave him complete authority over camera placements and lighting systems (quoted in Seaton and Martin, 1982a, p. 8).

In fact, the German art director Alfred Junge was based at the Sheperd's Bush studio of Gainsborough's parent company Gaumont-British. But the fact remains that he was one of a number of European creative and technical personnel recruited by the British film industry during the 30s. The co-operation between Britain and Germany and fluid exchange of personnel were characteristic of the Film Europe movement, an active attempt by British producers to project British cinema as European cinema. It was treated with suspicion by many within the industry, who

International identity: E. A. Dupont's *Moulin Rouge* (1928)

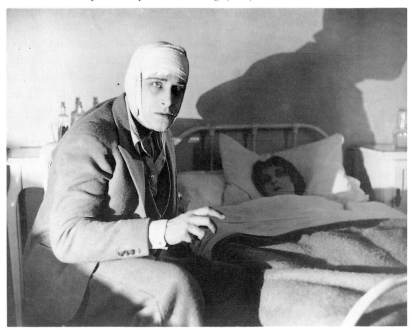

resented the foreign 'invasion', and by some film critics, who complained about lack of national specificity and about cultural colonisation.

As Higson points out, however, these suspicions were misplaced (Higson, 1993b). Although some European film-makers were in flight from Fascism, most of them came to Britain under contract and are better seen as pawns in the grand imperialist schemes of economic and cultural colonisation drawn up by British producers. Film Europe had a tremendous influence on 30s British cinema, particularly in the areas of art direction, cinematography and production, though its impact has scarcely been assessed. Clearly, it profoundly affected the visual style of British cinema, as well as its identity. Gainsborough, from its inception, was deeply implicated in the internationalist movement, involved in co-production deals with German companies and employing European directors and technical staff. A strange situation arose in which British directors, such as Alfred Hitchcock or Victor Saville, produced films which adopted European-influenced aesthetics, while European directors, such as the French-born Marcel Varnel and the Italian Monty Banks, were responsible for such quintessentially British efforts as the Will Hay comedies.

Film Europe, as an attempt to challenge Hollywood's hegemony, collapsed in the mid-30s. Yet its influence as a multi-cultural movement which stressed the interdependence of national cultures and cinemas persisted. That influence can be seen in the internationalism of 40s Powell and Pressburger, and in the Gainsborough costume cycle, which very clearly has (more than) one foot in Europe and another in Hollywood. It may have been partly this hybrid identity that so ennervated those quality critics fixated on cultural specificity. But it is also the case that by the mid- to late 30s, expressionism, which was identified by many with German cinema, had become a contaminated aesthetic. The wartime intensification of debates about how to construct an authentic national cinema revolved obsessively around the national/international axis − too great an emphasis on the former smacked of National Socialism, while the latter raised the familiar ghosts of invasion and colonialism.

This, then, is the highly volatile context in which the Gainsborough costume dramas should be seen. At the time of their release, they played a central role in arguments about national identity and cinema, which the opprobrium heaped on them then and their relative marginalisation since have helped to obscure. They were the other side of the coin to the consensus films, which were defined in terms of realism, authenticity and

Shades of Europe: *I Know Where I'm Going!* (1945)

ordinary people in contemporary settings. The realist quality canon could not have existed without these scurrilously inauthentic movies against which the critics defined the terms of a national cinema.

Significantly, the costume cycle was born out of conflict – between Edward Black, who took over day to day running of the studio after Balcon left to go to MGM in 1936, and Maurice Ostrer, who was in overall charge. By all accounts (Seaton and Martin, 1982b, p. 17; Murphy, 1983), Ted Black, a no-nonsense northerner with a shrewd populist touch, is the unsung hero of British cinema of the late 30s and early 40s; it was he who ensured that Gainsborough survived in this difficult period. Black ran a tight ship, producing popular, medium-budget comedies drawing on British music-hall traditions, from Will Hay to the Crazy Gang. Other successful productions included the historical film, *Tudor Rose* (Robert Stevenson, 1936), and Carol Reed's *Bank Holiday* (1938), which featured up and coming actress Margaret Lockwood, who went on to star in Hitchcock's *The Lady Vanishes* (1939) and to play a prominent role in many of the costume dramas. One of Black's many achievements had been to build up a stable of British stars, including Lockwood, Phyllis Calvert, Stewart Granger, James Mason, Patricia Roc *et al.*, and there is no doubt that this contributed to Gainsborough's success.

Black was predominantly concerned with the domestic market – particularly, it seems, with midlands and northern working-class audiences. There was no way that his films could compete with the grand internationalist aspirations of Alexander Korda's London Films, for example. In 1941, J. Arthur Rank acquired Gaumont-British and with it Gainsborough to add to his burgeoning collection of studios. Though at first Gainsborough was left to its own devices, there was a definite sea change, signalled by the production of two very different projects: Launder and Gilliat's *Millions Like Us* (1943) and the first of the costume cycle, *The Man in Grey* (Leslie Arliss, 1943). The populist realism of the former could hardly have been more at odds with the latter's dark themes of sexuality, class and betrayal, and though both films did well, the costume film was extremely successful at the box-office (Lant, 1991, pp. 231–3). Maurice Ostrer, previously a background figure, had initiated *The Man in Grey* against Black's judgment, and became increasingly intolerant of Black's enthusiasm for populist fare. The crunch apparently came over *Waterloo Road* (Sidney Gilliat, 1944), eventually released to commercial and critical approval in 1945. Ostrer, backed by Rank, won the battle. Black resigned and joined Korda at MGM, while Ostrer assembled a new team consisting of producers Harold Huth and R. J. Minney to launch the cycle of melodramas and costume dramas in what was to be the studio's most commercially successful phase.

The dispute between Black and Ostrer is illuminating, since it was not just about box-office success – although that was certainly a factor in Ostrer's desire to produce more costume dramas. Black's projects did well at the box office, and continued to do so after his departure. The disagreement was probably something to do with class and politics: Ostrer was a Churchill supporter with little time for Black's populist leanings. But it was also to do with the status of spectacle, fantasy and internationalism in British cinema, and renewed attempts by Rank to compete with Hollywood (Murphy, 1992, p. 220). By 1943, the year *The Man in Grey* was released, Britain was looking forward to the end of the war. Ostrer, along with others writing in the trade press, claimed that a new mood was abroad in the country, and that audiences wanted escapism rather than realism and contemporary subjects. While prestigious quality companies such as Two Cities continued to produce realist films, a thread of fantasy and exoticism began to surface in British cinema, to the horror of those critics who felt that during the war years Britain had achieved a mature, quality cinema to rival any in the world (Murphy, 1988). As already indicated, this quality cinema was generally more successful with critics and official agencies than with audiences. Maurice Ostrer had judged the popular mood accurately. The Gainsborough costume cycle was clearly part of this trend towards fantasy.

The distinction between realism and fantasy is difficult to maintain in relation to fiction. Certainly, the realist consensus films contained elements of fantasy and melodrama, while fantasy films addressed contemporary issues, albeit in disguise, as Sue Harper has put it (Harper, 1988). The costume cycle, for example, as well as dealing with relevant questions of women's sexual desires and class mobility, is centrally concerned with national identity. Indeed, it is remarkable how dark a vision of British society many of them project. It is often suggested that this is made possible by their being set in the past, at a safe distance. I have already indicated that in costume romance the past is anything but a safe place, and the hysterical response of critics to the Gainsborough costume films would seem to support this view. What the costume dramas set out to do, I would argue, is exorcise the past and rehearse the future. They look back to a time of class, sexual and ethnic inequality, and uncontrolled male abuse of power, in order to look forward to a more egalitarian future in which the role of women will be crucial. In doing so, they present a picture of a nation in crisis, with shifting and unstable boundaries. In this sense, they could be said to be closer to the true state of Britain during the war and immediately post-war than the realist consensus films with their emphasis on stable, coherent identities.

However, it is not my intention to rehabilitate the costume dramas into a revisionist pantheon. Nor do I want to suggest that they are in any way representative of British cinema of the period. I am primarily interested in what they can tell us, as part of the general picture of 40s British cinema, about ideas surrounding national identity then and now. I have already spent some time indicating ways in which the costume films offended against the official criteria of quality and authenticity governing the consensus movies. I'd now like to turn to the films themselves and look in more detail at their representation of Britishness.

I've chosen, for the purposes of argument, to look at four costume dramas which feature narratives set in European locales, cross-cultural and/or cross-class romance and, most important, an identity crisis in a central protagonist. None of these elements is particularly unusual in British cinema of the period. There was a general move to widen the scope of what constituted Britishness by incorporating regional characters into the narrative, and to soften chauvinism by reassessing national attitudes to our European allies (Ealing's *Johnny Frenchman*, Charles Frend, 1945, is a good example). It is also noticeable that European languages, particularly French, were spoken in British films of the time more frequently than they are today, often without subtitles. British Europhobia was temporarily put to one side as the British imagined themselves overcoming cultural differences with the Other, or at least some of the Other. To be British could also mean being European – national identity could be multiple.

However, there are key differences in the costume romances' depiction of this *rapprochement*. In the realist films, for example, British characters remain first and foremost British. Their values may be challenged, even modified by contact with other cultures, but this tolerance and flexibility is seen as an essentially British quality anyway. In the costume dramas, British identity is deeply in crisis, seriously at risk of being swallowed up by the European Other. The interesting thing is that this Other, and the qualities that make it Other, are given an unusual amount of space and value. The costume films deal in fantasies of loss of identity. They suggest that identity itself is fluid and unstable, like the costume genre itself, a hybrid state or form. And they suggest that national identity is not pure, but mixed.

In line with the general softening of attitudes towards certain 'foreign' cultures, cross-cultural romance also featured strongly in many wartime films. A common theme was the sexual sophistication and allure of the foreigner in comparison to the repressed British. While this sustained certain negative, 'exotic' stereotypes, in many cases these stereotypes were turned on their heads by the positive value attached to exotic characters in both narrative and *mise en scène*. In the costume dramas, the negative characteristics of foreign protagonists are often redeemed by love and self-sacrifice, which renders them equal, if not superior, to British characters.

Not surprisingly, the theme of identity is particularly evident in wartime cinema. In wartime conditions, the undecidability of identity, whether of gender or nation comes to the fore. One is reminded of Antonia Lant's description of wartime gender slippage (Lant, 1991), and of Marjorie Garber's retelling of the anecdote about Hitler's panic when confronted with a caftan-clad Jew (Garber, 1992, p. 227). Secrecy, camouflage and disguise are essential in wartime for the protection of the nation, and if one adds to this the disguise of uniform effacing the boundaries of gender, then it is easy to see why the difficulty of determining who is who surfaces so often as a theme in wartime British cinema. Whereas in films with contemporary settings, the drama of mistaken identity and disguise is justified by the conditions of war (see, for example, *The Adventures of Tartu*, Harold S. Bucquet, 1943) and is usually unambiguously resolved, in the costume cycle, masquerade, and the multiple identities it implies, is closely linked to female desire, and the play of identity worked through by the costume narrative is either not resolved, or only ambiguously so.

The argument put forward by Garber that the fetishism, spectacle and display characteristic of masquerade and cross-dressing sustain the undecidability of gender is particularly relevant to the Gainsborough costume romances (Garber, 1992). Although in these movies fetishism is not nearly as marked as in Hollywood – Sternberg's films, for example – masquerade is a key factor in both narrative and visuals. It is also present in the spectacle of British stars playing French, Italian or Spanish characters, with little regard for authenticity: accents, costume and decor were as notoriously slippery in the depiction of place/geography as in the representation of period. While masquerade is important to all costume drama – the actors are clearly dressed up, 'playing' at being the characters they represent – its significance in costume romance has more to do with keeping open the play of identity. In the same way, the self-conscious and self-reflexive use of costume and decor emphasises fluidity and slippage, even when the narrative appears to have tied up the loose ends. The function of visual codes in commenting on and counteracting narrative has been explored in relation to melodrama, and the costume dramas are, of course, melodramas. However, I am more interested here in their symptomatic status in British cinema. The four costume dramas considered below bring into particularly sharp focus the crisis of identity at the heart of our national cinema.

Madonna of the Seven Moons (Arthur Crabtree, 1944), my first case study, is not strictly speaking a costume drama, since it is set in the late 30s; however, in all other respects it meets my criteria. Costume is central to its tale of frustrated female desire, and is used in a symbolic manner. Masquerade is both narrative theme and visual message, and is doubled and redoubled in the script. The story is set in Italy. Phyllis Calvert plays Maddalena, a wealthy and saint-like Italian matron who was raped by a peasant when young, with the result that she now suffers from blackouts during which, transformed by her gypsy clothes and earrings into Rosanna, she escapes from her long-suffering husband to the arms of her robber lover, Nino (played by Stewart Granger), who owns the Inn of the Seven Moons in a poor quarter of Florence. Maddalena has a daughter, Angela (Patricia Roc), who has been educated in England, and who has returned home with modern ideas which precipitate Maddalena's present crisis.

The release of Maddalena's pent-up sexual desire is explicitly provoked by a culture clash in which 'progressive' English attitudes to sexuality and gender are in conflict with Italian repression. Angela's modernising impulse extends to persuading her mother to dress in a more sophisticated manner and widen her social activities – the script has her choosing and trying out new outfits and hairstyles and throwing a party for Angela. It is precisely this move towards modernity that flings her back into the past and puts Angela in mortal danger. Madonna's story evinces a dilemma characteristic of costume romance: the past must be exorcised to make way for the future; but all too often the past is seen as a more exciting, adventurous prospect. Characters are tempted to linger there rather than move forward (remember Freud's 'compulsion to repeat').

The film's costume narrative underwrites this ambivalence. Angela's breezy, unisex modern image (reminiscent of women's masculinised wartime gear) is in stark contrast to the full skirts and decorative flounces donned by Maddalena as Rosanna. Similarly, Angela's egalitarian relationship with her boyfriend Evelyn (mistaken at first by her parents for a girl) is singularly lacking in passion in comparison to Rosanna's (no less equal) overtly sexual affair with Nino. The film looks backwards and forwards at once, questioning the validity of a democratic future without sexual adventure and danger, yet projecting the past as riven with crisis and conflict. Putting the past and future into crisis in this manner certainly would not have pleased those concerned with constructing and maintaining secure and coherent identities in wartime and post-war Britain. However, it may well have appealed to women whose place in national culture was uncertain and uneasy, and whose future was in question. Maddalena's symptoms are not just a response to modernity, a retreat into the past to avoid a lacklustre future; they represent a flight from home and motherhood and traditional femininity. As Rosanna, she experiences sexual power and freedom which her maternal role does not allow, and which are given positive validation by the script. Indeed, the intensity of adulterous sexual passion depicted in this film, and in *Caravan* (Arthur Crabtree, 1946), is remarkable for British cinema of the period.

The costume narrative clearly signals Maddalena's desire to escape the confines of hearth and home. Her transformation into Rosanna is marked by the shedding of her matronly garb and the donning of what can only be described as gypsy gear. Thus exotically kitted out, her personality and body language completely change: as Sue Harper has pointed out, this is a key example of designer Haffenden's symbolic use of costume to signify emotional and sexual themes and states of mind (Harper, 1983). It can also be seen as an instance of conscious disregard for authenticity in favour of employing costume as a complex signifier in its own right – precisely the kind of obtrusive role for design that directors such as Alfred Hitchcock apparently abhorred (see Gaines and Herzog, 1990).

Rosanna's lover Nino and his family are not gypsies; on the contrary, although they are thieves and confidence tricksters who rip off the rich and are not averse to rape and murder, they own a tavern (albeit a disreputable one). Thus, Rosanna's gypsy costume has no meaning other

Past and future in crisis: *Madonna of the Seven Moons*

Who am I, where am I?: Phylis Calvert in *Madonna of the Seven Moons*

than to represent her own itinerant spirit, her urge to cross boundaries of time and place and elude the role allotted to her. The gypsy costume is a disguise or masquerade which allows Rosanna/Maddalena to try out different aspects of herself. It represents freedom and escape, as well as exoticism. Rosanna's gypsy persona, and her 'other life' are strongly validated, as I have already indicated. But masquerade and its attendant identity confusion turn out to have tragic consequences. On carnival night, when everyone is in disguise, Nino's brother Sandro, who has designs on Angela, lures her to the tavern with the promise that she will find her errant mother there. He drugs her and takes her upstairs with the intention of raping her. He is prevented from doing so by Rosanna, who arrives in vengeful mood, believing that Sandro is Nino making love to another woman (the brothers are both dressed in harlequin costume). Rosanna stabs Sandro and is stabbed in return, but not before she has recognised Angela and become Maddalena once more. Hot on the trail of Angela, Evelyn and his English friend – ineffectual as ever – arrive too late to prevent Maddalena's death. But if Maddalena's identity crisis is brought to an abrupt and brutal end by the script, the costume narrative keeps her dual persona in play. She dies with the symbols of her conflicting desires on her body: the cross and the rose.

If *Madonna*'s costume narrative speaks its own language, the art direction is equally autonomous. Andrew Mazzei's rich rococo interiors in the Labardi mansion in Rome are neither appropriate to the 30s period nor to the sexual repression which seems to characterise Maddalena's marriage. Instead, they look forward (or back) to the eighteenth-century garden where Rosanna makes love with Nino. The effect is of a time warp: although apparently set in the late 30s, the sense is of being transported into a fictionalised, eroticised past. Like Maddalena, the audience of the day was encouraged to travel through time and place and to lose themselves in the realms of fantasy. In the process, they were invited to question who and where they were – in other words, to problematise their own sexual and national identities. The studio's promotional strategies emphasised this experience of entering a different world. According to the press material held by the British Film Institute,

Carnival time: Stewart Granger in *Madonna of the Seven Moons*

cinema managers were encouraged to dress their usherettes in costumes reflecting the gypsy theme of *Caravan*, while for the release of *The Magic Bow*, an outsized violin was put on display outside one cinema.

The sequence of Rosanna's death described above is a good example of *Madonna*'s indebtedness to 'expressionist' aesthetics. As Rosanna climbs the tavern stairs to confront Sandro/Nino, the high-contrast, chiaroscuro lighting, looming architectural shapes and pounding music lend the scene a doom-laden emotional intensity. The moment when the drama of mistaken identity is unravelled is played with melodramatic excess, using extreme close-ups. Nothing could be further from the aesthetic restraint advocated by the champions of realist quality cinema. But more than this, *Madonna of the Seven Moons* projects a 'foreign' look, a swirling amalgam of European styles from rococo to Gothic to expressionism, within which the British preference for the undecorated and the perpendicular is quite submerged. (Pevsner, 1956, identifies two traditions in English art: the plain and perpendicular, and the decorative. The latter, however, he sees as having been subordinated to the former.)

I do not need to labour the gender implications of such decorative excess. *Madonna*'s aesthetics were doubly threatening to the criteria of 40s consensus cinema: not only overwhelmingly feminine but also chaotically 'foreign'. Such flamboyance, though inspired by European styles, was also too close to Hollywood for comfort (the 'Europeanism' of Hollywood is a subject ripe for investigation). Haffenden's overtly sexualised costume designs were a far cry from consensus British cinema's insistence on deglamorised heroines (see Lant, 1991), reasserting the femininity that wartime conditions had submerged. It was not a question of reinscribing the boundaries of sexual difference, which is how many of those who objected to the New Look saw it. It was rather a reaffirmation of the feminine principle, in relation to men as well as women. As I have already argued, the New Look was an androgynous style that favoured a feminised rather than masculinised ambiguity. Women who felt themselves empowered by being treated as equal to men (though just how much this actually happened is open to question – see Harper, 1988) were naturally reluctant to relinquish their freedoms, and saw the return to femininity as a retreat. But the New Look, like Haffenden's costumes for the Gainsborough cycle, projected femininity as powerful, and herein lies the secret of its scandalous transgression.

Caravan (1946), unlike *Madonna of the Seven Moons*, is set in England in the 19th century, but, like *Madonna*, it was directed by ex-cinematographer Arthur Crabtree. Stewart Granger plays Richard, an impoverished

Femininity as powerful: costume designers Elizabeth Haffenden (left) and Joan Bridge

writer of mixed parentage in that his doctor father married a woman with gypsy blood. He is in love with an English woman, Oriana (Anne Crawford), from an aristocratic family whose debts put her at the mercy of the unscrupulous aristocrat Francis (Dennis Price) who, like Richard, has loved Oriana from childhood. Oriana and Richard plan to marry, but before this can happen, Richard accepts a commission in Spain from a Spanish nobleman whose life he has saved. Francis secretly arranges for Richard to be killed in Spain, but he is saved by Rosal (Jean Kent), a gypsy dancer. Rosal takes the amnesiac Richard to her mountain cave to live with her. Believing him to be dead, Oriana marries Francis,' who turns out to be morally and sexually corrupt. When she discovers that Richard is alive, Oriana travels to Spain, followed by Francis and his effeminate sidekick Wycroft, who again try to murder Richard. Rosal steps between them and is killed by the bullet intended for Richard. In an extraordinary finale, in which Francis disappears into a patch of quicksand that Richard had earlier survived, Richard saves Oriana and they return to England and happiness.

Clearly, this narrative can be subsumed into parochial notions of national identity. Richard's encounter with a foreign culture, in the form of the exotic Rosal, puts not just his life, but his Englishness in peril. The return to England and Oriana appears to be a renunciation of his dalliance with all things Spanish and a reaffirmation of 'home'. I do not wish to deny this possible interpretation, which may well have been what the scriptwriters had in mind. But it can only be held together at the cost of ignoring the film's visual and auditory levels, where it is obvious that something else is going on – and one can be reasonably certain that the art and costume departments were aware of the effects they were creating. The relationship between 'England' and 'Spain' projected by *Caravan* is more complex than the narrative implies. The pattern one might expect, whereby British values are tested, then cleansed of contamination by those of other cultures in order to be affirmed, is substantially reversed.

Negative and positive values are distributed between both cultures: Francis and Wycroft's villainy is mirrored in the Spanish gypsy gang that attacks Richard, but Richard's heroism is reflected in Rosal's self-sacrifice, which saves his life. The English aristocracy, represented by Francis, is shown as weak and corrupt – in other words, Britain's ruling class must be cleansed of such elements, not surprisingly, by an upstanding bourgeois hero. But the Spanish nobleman Don Carlos who supports Richard's aspirations to be a writer is entirely honourable, and Rosal's gypsy heritage (she comes from a particular tribe with its own code of honour) is represented positively. Indeed, a considerable amount of time and space is given over to 'Spanish' music and dancing in *Caravan*. It does not matter that these renditions are not authentic – or rather, it matters in the sense that it is made clear that it is an *idea* of Spain that is being presented. Thus, national identity is specifically offered as construct, as myth.

Caravan does project Spain as dangerous terrain. The exoticism and sexual allure that captivate Richard threaten to swallow him up completely – hence the quicksand image, not to mention the womb-like cave in which he and Rosal live. But the sheer vibrancy and sense of freedom of movement in the Spanish scenes contrast vividly with the cramped, closed darkness of the English sequences. (It is significant that *Caravan* included some outdoor location shooting in the Welsh countryside for the Spanish scenes; this was unusual at the time because filming in the studio was cheaper.) Oriana comes off badly in comparison with Rosal's courage and seductive sexuality, even in the final scenes where she attempts to win Richard back and clear his name. Rosal's contemptuous question 'What do you cold English women know of love?', ridiculed by contemporary critics (see Aspinall and Murphy, 1983, p. 75), actually carries a lot of weight in the light of the passionate intensity of her sexual relationship with Richard, which is presented with extreme frankness.

Although Spain can never represent 'home' to Richard – once an Englishman always an Englishman – it does offer a great deal that

England does not. The visual codes back this up. Elizabeth Haffenden's exquisite costume designs for Rosal's dance sequences reveal her body and emphasise her sinuous movements. Her rustling skirts, the shiny pieces of glittering metal with which they are decorated and the tinkling bells of her tambourine all transmit sexual energy and power, while her

Gypsy spirit: Jean Kent in *Caravan*

An Englishman in peril: Stewart Granger in *Caravan*

performances suggest skill and professional pride as well as eroticism. By contrast, Oriana's clothes are fussy and restrictive, though occasionally more *décolleté* than might be expected. At a certain point, a Spanish influence in Oriana's dress becomes evident, implying that Spanish femininity has something to teach English women. Certainly, after

Oriana's experiences of rape and imprisonment in her marriage to Francis, Spain seems to offer freedom and independence denied to Victorian English women.

John Bryan's set designs confirm the restrictiveness of English life. In the early childhood sequences, told from Richard's perspective in flashback, even the English countryside appears closed in; it is very obviously shot in the studio. The city streets look equally studio-bound, while the Victorian interiors are dark and claustrophobic, even in Don Carlos's roomy mansion. In Spain, the spatial relationships and light are quite different. The countryside is frequently shot on location, giving a sense of wildness and openness. The interiors and garden of Don Carlos's Spanish house are elegant, spacious and brightly lit, while the tavern where Rosal performs is a huge cavernous room constructed from arches carved out of ancient stone, centring on a wide, curved staircase and large circular area where the dancing takes place. Even the darker confines of Rosal's cave, where she nurses Richard back to health, are mitigated by being set in

Freedom abroad: Stewart Granger and Jean Kent in *Caravan*

Elizabeth Haffenden's sketches for Anne Crawford's dresses in the *Caravan* press book

mountain countryside near to a clear, sparkling lake in which she swims naked.

All this quite consciously signals that freedom is to be found elsewhere than in England – not exactly a welcome message for those concerned with projecting a post-war vision of British liberal democracy. But *Caravan*'s message is yet more complex. It is Richard's superior knowledge of the foreign terrain after his Spanish escapade that enables him to destroy the villain Francis, a truly reprehensible specimen of Englishness: murderer, thief, rapist, coward and more besides. In other words, Richard's identity crisis, and by implication his mixed origins, are a positive force in cleansing Englishness and restoring equilibrium. This represents an interesting reversal of the principle of ethnic cleansing. There could hardly be a more positive affirmation of the virtues of mixed identity, or of the cultural value of exile and return. And the audiences who travelled with Richard in his return to his maternal roots may well have viewed their homeland a little differently after the journey.

Both *Madonna* and *Caravan* attach positive value to the itinerant gypsy spirit at the heart of the costume romances. The prominence of gypsies in popular fiction of the 30s and 40s (see Light, 1992, p. 157) can, as Sue Harper has argued, be seen as a way of giving recognition to marginal groups, whose threat to society is then neutralised (Harper, 1988). This may be true in some cases – in the Cineguild costume drama *Blanche Fury* (Marc Allegret, 1947), for example, gypsies are seen as a dangerous, contaminating force. But I think there is more to the gypsy phenomenon than a fascination with the marginal and the exotic. Gypsies are travellers who transgress boundaries of nation and property. They have little or no stake in national identity, and they are ethnically mixed. They are nomadic, which means that 'home', in the sense of a place to which they belong, is never more than a temporary dwelling. In escapist literature, which depends on fantasies of travelling to all kinds of new shores, 'gypsyness' can represent the positive advantages of freedom from the shackles of normal, respectable society. In the extraordinary *Wings of the Morning* (Harold Schuster, 1936), for example, a convoluted story of cross-dressing and gender disturbance reminiscent of *Sylvia Scarlett* (George Cukor, 1935), gypsies are central to the drama of mixed and mistaken identities.

In the Gainsborough costume cycle, gypsies are depicted not as social outcasts, but as central figures in what is essentially a mobile society. Characters travel between home and abroad, between past and present, and even – as in the case of *Jassy* (Bernard Knowles, 1947), in which

Margaret Lockwood plays a gypsy – from the bottom to the top of the social ladder. Such an emphasis on mobility, particularly when it came to women, could prove troublesome to official agencies, as Antonia Lant has pointed out (Lant, 1991). Whereas the realist consensus films managed an uneasy compromise between mobility and stability, the Gainsborough costume romances displayed no such compunctions, consciously celebrating the gypsy spirit, above all on the visual level, and minimising any attendant anxieties.

In *Caravan*, a fictional Spain is used to project a fantasy, both troubling and exciting, that England might benefit from being 'Europeanised'. In *The Magic Bow* (1946), directed by Bernard Knowles and based on a novel about the life of virtuoso violinist Nicolo Paganini, the period and European setting are used as a mask for exploring the difficulties and possibilities of cross-class and cross-cultural romance. Although clearly a fictionalised account, the film was damned by critics for its lack of authenticity, particularly because it presented a cleaned-up version of Paganini's sexual exploits (Aspinall and Murphy, 1983, p. 77). In looking

Contaminated: Stewart Granger in *Blanche Fury*

104

What a mix-up: *Wings of the Morning*

for greater realism, the critics seemed to be asking for a more robustly censorious view of the Italian musician. In a book about Hollywood bio-pics, George F. Custen has argued that they perform the function of constructing from personal life histories a larger history of the nation (Custen, 1992). As with all historical film, accuracy is very important, although a certain amount of leeway is allowed, and certain strategies, such as the inclusion of historical documentation, are employed to bolster the effect of authenticity. Custen also claims that Hollywood bio-pics of famous foreigners are generally used to show America in a better light than the protagonist's country of origin.

The Magic Bow fails on all these counts. Apart from offering a 'flexible' account of Paganini's life, its sense of period is characteristically elastic, while England comes off badly in comparison to the cultivation of the French and the Italians (there are sniping references to a national failure to appreciate music, for example). The story is set in Italy during the Napoleonic wars and concerns a love affair between Jeanne, a French aristocratic woman played by Phyllis Calvert, and the impoverished Paganini (Stewart Granger). The couple battle against class and cultural differences until finally they are united. The film is centred on a comparison between France and Italy, in which the former is seen as rigidly hierarchical, ruled by a dictatorial emperor, and the latter as more open to social mobility, governed by a benevolent Pope. Paganini and his entourage work their way up the social ladder until he is given a knighthood, which puts him on an equal footing with Jeanne and enables them to marry – a victory over the social restrictions which have kept them apart.

Andrew Mazzei and John Bryan's set designs are impressive, contrasting the humble simplicity of Paganini's Genoese house with the resplendent halls of Jeanne's mansion in Parma or the magnificence of the Vatican. Yet in spite of the narrative's endorsement of upward mobility, costume and art direction tell a different story. The film's visual codes emphasise social constraint, from the early scene in which Paganini is filmed through the bars of a prison as his music helps an internee escape, to the horizontal shadows of the shutters falling on him as he plays the violin when Jeanne leaves. Haffenden's costumes pick up the theme: as Paganini, his 'companion' Bianchi (Jean Kent) and manager Germi (Cecil

Mobile woman: Margaret Lockwood in *Jassy*

106

Economical with the truth: *The Magic Bow*

Parker) become rich, their clothes become more elaborate and restrictive, and their body movements stiffer. Haffenden uses stripe motifs to echo the prison bars, suggesting that the entry into high society is a step towards bondage. In this way, the film manages to celebrate social mobility while simultaneously honouring Paganini's lower-class origins. Those origins are further sanctioned by a contrast between the soft curves (echoing the shape of the violin) of the decor in the Paganini home and the Parma rooming house, and the towering, perpendicular architecture and geometric patterns of the mansions and palaces of the nobility.

Stewart Granger's feminised, eroticised image played an important part in the marketing of both *Caravan* and *The Magic Bow*. In the press material held by the British Film Institute, while the text stresses Granger's acting ability and athletic prowess, the images present him as an exotic figure – indeed, there are resonances of the ethnic and sexual ambiguity associated with Rudolph Valentino. In both films, the crisis of national identity is intimately linked to masculinity crisis (in *The Magic*

Bow, Paganini's obsession with Jeanne causes him to lose his ability to play the violin and to be haunted by fears of failure). And in both films, period costume is used to reveal and emphasise Granger's physical attributes (as, indeed, it was throughout his career, when he was scarcely ever out of tights and cutaway jackets). In *Caravan*, his clothing draws comments from other characters, and his transformation into Spanish gypsy is signalled by his dressing up in skimpy matador costume which reveals his torso from the waist down and which he refers to as 'draughty'. (In this sequence he is also seen doing the cooking – further evidence of his feminisation.) Granger's Spanish garb is highly decorative and provokes the more soberly dressed Francis to comment on his tailor.

In *The Magic Bow*, Paganini's upward mobility is marked by a change from simple dress – soft white blouse, tight dark jacket and hose – to more formal, decorative gear, until in the final sequence he is resplendent in a heavily embroidered jacket. As suggested by Marjorie Garber, such 'virile display' has a feminising effect, overshadowing phallic power with

Upward bound: Jean Kent, Cecil Parker and Stewart Granger in *The Magic Bow*

108

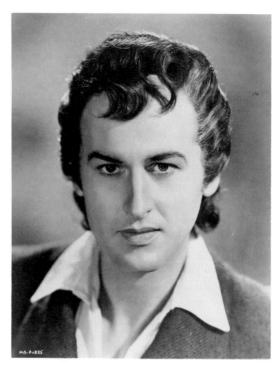

Exoticised and eroticised: Stewart Granger in *The Magic Bow*

what it attempts to repress, and revealing that no one has the phallus (Garber, 1992, p. 355). In these costume romances, the heroes' encounters with foreign cultures often involve a parallel assimilation of feminine qualities – another indication of the films' affirmation of the feminine principle and, perhaps, another reason for the critics' disapprobation.

The positive value attached to mixed identities in the Gainsborough costume romances did not last long. Soon after the war, the optimism and forward-looking egalitarianism projected by most wartime British films degenerated into introspective gloom, exemplified by the transition from the ebullient, colourful jingoism of Olivier's *Henry V* (Laurence Olivier, 1945) to the black and white melancholy of his *Hamlet* (Laurence Olivier, 1948). At the end of 1946, Sydney Box took over from Maurice Ostrer as head of Gainsborough, and the films subsequently produced by the studio had a much darker tone. Significantly, Box was obsessed with authenticity, and his attempts to inject verisimilitude into the Gainsborough costume films and melodramas are well documented. All the historical research and period detail that went into films such as *Christopher Columbus* (David MacDonald, 1949) and *The Bad Lord Byron* (David MacDonald, 1949) did not, however, win the favour of the contemporary critics. They found the results dull and unconvincing: the search for authenticity, as ever, was a lost cause (Aspinall and Murphy, 1983, pp. 64, 88, 90).

The concern with verisimilitude coincided with a closing down in the costume dramas of celebration of hybrid identities: Europe became a site of xenophobic fears once more. This is well illustrated by the film which is generally taken to mark the end of the Gainsborough costume cycle: *So Long at the Fair* (1950), directed by Terence Fisher and Anthony Darnborough. The former went on to work for Hammer, where the British costume genre resurfaced in the late 50s and 60s. In this film, the innocent English heroine Vicky Barton (Jean Simmons) visits Paris with her brother Johnny (David Tomlinson) in 1889, the year of the Exposition, a major celebration of French national identity. Vicky, unlike the sceptical Johnny, is seduced by the colourful beauty and excitement of Paris, but soon discovers that it is all a facade. When her brother and his hotel room both disappear, she enlists the help of George, a young British painter (Dirk Bogarde) and together they break into Johnny's room, which has been sealed up, and through the plastered-over door into the hallway, effectively smashing through the deceptive veneer of Frenchness. In fact, Vicky's brother has contracted bubonic plague and been

Elizabeth Haffenden's sketches in *The Magic Bow* press book

Fashions in "The Magic Bow"

Feminine display: fashion tie-ins for *The Magic Bow*

spirited away by the hotel manageress Mme Hervé to a nearby convent, a remarkably pessimistic view of the consequences of consorting with Europeans.

So Long at the Fair redraws the boundaries of gender and national identity which the earlier costume romances had so dauntlessly dissolved. In this film, the English characters' perilous encounter with a foreign, European culture is not eroticised, but imbued with a doom-laden vision of contamination. The visual codes play a significant part in marking the line between Englishness (as authenticity) and Frenchness (as fraud). The verisimilitude of the film-makers' paranoid depiction of Paris is emphasised by extensive location shooting in and around the city streets. The English stars, Bogarde, Simmons and Tomlinson, play English characters and, in spite of the Parisian setting, the story is

Anglo-centric. Cultural difference, rather than *rapprochement*, is stressed. The English (apart from Bogarde, who has lived in Paris for some time and knows his way around) have difficulty in understanding the French language, and since much of the dialogue is spoken in French without subtitles, many in the audience may well have been in the same position. Apart from adding authenticity to the production, this hindrance to effective communication underlines the deceptive nature of the French.

The art direction, by George Provis and Cedric Dawe, confirms rather than counteracts this perception. Paris is represented as lush and highly decorative, from the tree-lined streets prettily dappled with sunlight to the hotel interiors, exquisitely ornamented – almost to excess, particularly in the concierge's parlour. Haffenden's costumes seem primarily concerned with period accuracy and with delineating between masculinity and femininity: the men, even the 'artistic' Bogarde, are soberly dressed, while the women are elaborately decked out in Victorian bustles, pleats and furls which echo the overdressed interiors and labyrinthine corridors of the French hotel. The association of spectacle, excess and display with foreignness and femininity serves to emphasise the masculi-

Redrawing boundaries: Dirk Bogarde and Jean Simmons in *So Long at the Fair*

French duplicity: Dirk Bogarde in *So Long at the Fair*

nised virtues of restraint and honesty characterising Britishness. Significantly for my argument, when Vicky dons the masquerade costume which will help her and George to unravel the mystery of the missing hotel room, it is one of classical-style simplicity, in sharp contrast to the ostentatious frills and flounces she wore previously. It is as though she has shed her Parisian finery in order to rediscover her true national identity. The deception that typifies masquerade is only justified in this case because it enables the truth to come to light. Whereas in the earlier Gainsborough costume romances, masquerade facilitated the play of identities, in *So Long at the Fair* it works to consolidate authentic identities.

So Long at the Fair is deeply xenophobic – there can hardly be a stronger deterrent to venturing outside England than the fear of falling prey to the black death – yet it does comment on English xenophobia at the same time. Johnny's derogatory remarks about France and his offensive behaviour towards the hotel staff are echoed in Mrs O'Donovan's refusal to speak anything but English while in Paris, and in her philistine response to George's Impressionist-influenced paintings. In a sense, then, xenophobia is presented as a self-fulfilling prophecy – certainly in Johnny's case, since his reflections on the likelihood of being poisoned in the Montmartre cafes prefigure his subsequent near-fatal illness. This, and the uncanniness at the centre of the plot (the disappearance of Johnny and his hotel room has no rational explanation at first) make it possible for the film to be interpreted as a discourse on the process of constructing national identity and on the tension between the *heimlich* and *unheimlich* (uncanny) in identity formation (see Chapters II and III above). It is interesting that David Pirie sees *So Long at the Fair* as a prototype for the vampire films that Fisher went on to direct for Hammer (Pirie, 1973, pp. 53–5). Count Dracula certainly qualifies as an uncanny 'boundary phenomenon' haunting the permeable borders of bourgeois British society; the creeping black death (reflected in the black clothes and bizarre behaviour of concierge Mme Hervé and her effeminate brother Narcisse) that attacks Johnny Barton carries similar significance.

But if *So Long at the Fair* can be seen as a meditation on xenophobia on one level, it nevertheless resolves matters unambiguously in favour of pure, authentic identities. When Vicky and George finally discover the truth behind Johnny's disappearance, what is revealed is the necessity for looking beyond deceptive surfaces if pollution by other cultures is to be avoided. The film's conclusion is profoundly pessimistic: Vicky finds her brother, but his survival is uncertain. Vicky and George leave the convent shrouded in melancholy, a resolution which allows little hope for future Anglo-European encounters.

So Long at the Fair encapsulates the struggle between authenticity/ realism and fantasy in British cinema of the 40s, a struggle in which, as I have argued, much was at stake, including the future of British cinema as a national/international venture. These issues were part of wider cultural debates about national identity in wartime and post-war Britain, and in this context it is hardly surprising that films should have been made, both inside and outside realist consensus cinema, which tested the boundaries of Britishness. It is more surprising that subsequent commentators on the period should have concentrated so overwhelmingly on the consensus films in discussions of national identity. This betrays a deep-seated reluctance to break the consensus on British cinema, even among revisionist historians. I have tried to indicate some of the reasons behind this reluctance by exploring the attachment to authentic identities which pervades even the more progressive critical approaches. It is this attachment which, I believe, has contributed to the marginalisation of the blatantly inauthentic Gainsborough costume dramas and the consequent impoverishment of debate.

But it is also the particular combination of femininity, foreignness and inauthenticity which puts the costume romances beyond the pale. The negative response of so many critics is symptomatic of a cultural strategy which devalues these categories in order to shore up a masculinised notion of identity. By implication, the reassessment of British cinema is intimately linked to a revaluation of femininity. The costume romances, which reinscribe the feminine principle into history, are central to that process. But they also, because of their emphasis on hybrid identities and concern with crossing national borders, encourage a less parochial view of British cinema, one which is more transgressive and adventurous, dedicated to venturing beyond fixed boundaries. The Gainsborough costume dramas' focus on exile and return, their play on the shifts of identity which are central to pleasure in cinema, make travellers of us all.

APPENDIX

(Credits compiled from the prints, and press material held by the BFI. Dates taken from Salmi, 1982.)

Madonna of the Seven Moons (1944)
Production Company: *Gainsborough*, Director: *Arthur Crabtree*, In Charge of Production: *Maurice Ostrer*, Producer: *R. J. Minney*, Associate Producer: *R. E. Dearing*, Production Manager: *Harold Richmond*, Script: *Roland Pertwee*, Scenario Editor: *Brock Williams*, Based on the novel: *The Madonna of Seven Moons*, by Margery Lawrence, Director of Photography: *Jack Cox*, Editor: *Lito Carruthers*, Art director: *Andrew Mazzei*, Musical Director: *Louis Levy*, Incidental Music: *Hans May*, Costumes: *Elizabeth Haffenden*, Sound Supervisor: *B. C. Sewell*, Religious Adviser: *Father Carey*

Cast
Phyllis Calvert *Maddalena Labardi/Rosanna*, Stewart Granger *Nino Barucci*, Patricia Roc *Angela Labardi*, Peter Glenville *Sandro Barucci*, John Stuart *Giuseppe Labardi*, Reginald Tate *Ackroyd*, Peter Murray Hill *Logan*, Dulcie Gray *Nesta*, Alan Hames *Evelyn*, Hilda Bayley *Mrs Fiske*, Evelyn Darvell *Millie*, Nancy Price *Mama Barucci*, Jean Kent *Vittoria*, Amy Veness *Tessa*, Robert Speaight *Priest*, Eliot Makeham *Bossi*, Danny Green *Scorpi*, Helen Haye *Mother Superior*

Florence, 1919. After being raped by a peasant, Maddalena leaves the Convent of the Sacred Heart to be married to the wealthy Giuseppi Labardi, a friend of her father's. Soon afterwards, their daughter Angela is born. Angela is sent away to be educated in England. She returns home to Rome with her English boyfriend Evelyn, who is in the diplomatic service. Maddalena leads a saintly and reclusive life, and is disturbed by Angela's modern ideas and dress. Angela encourages Maddalena to buy sophisticated clothes and to throw a party to celebrate Angela's birthday. At the party, Maddalena faints at the sight of Sandro Barucci, a gigolo who has designs on Angela. That night, Maddalena dresses in gypsy clothes and, taking her jewellery, goes to Florence. It transpires that Maddalena has disappeared before, on one occasion for a whole year.

Maddalena, now Rosanna, makes her way to the Inn of the Seven Moons to rejoin her cutpurse lover Nino Barucci, who owns the tavern. They enjoy a passionate reunion. Meanwhile, Angela sets out to find her mother through the missing jewellery. The trail leads her to Florence, where she joins forces with Evelyn's artist friend Logan and his wife Nesta. They meet Sandro, Nino's brother, who offers to help Angela in her search. He agrees to take her to the Inn of the Seven Moons the following night, when a carnival will be under way. At the same time, Nino and his gang plan to raid the Labardi house in Florence, which has just been reopened. On carnival night, Nino, Sandro and the gang all dress in harlequin costume to confuse the police. Sandro brings Angela to the tavern and drugs her, taking her upstairs with the intention of raping her.

Meanwhile, Evelyn returns from England and, learning that Angela is with Sandro, sets out with Logan to find her. Rosanna returns to the tavern, where she mistakes Sandro for Nino and, believing him to be making love to a rival, stabs him before he can rape Angela. Sandro stabs Rosanna in return. Angela confronts her mother, who recognises her and collapses. Evelyn and Logan arrive, and Rosanna/Maddalena is taken back to the Labardi house. Nino discovers Sandro's body and goes to the Labardi house with the intention of killing Giuseppe and reclaiming Rosanna. When he sees that Rosanna is dying and learns that she is married to Giuseppe, he turns away, leaving a rose, the symbol of their love, on Rosanna's breast.

Caravan (1946)
Production Company: *Gainsborough*, Director: *Arthur Crabtree*, Executive Producer: *Maurice Ostrer*, Producer: *Harold Huth*, Production Supervisor: *Albert Fennell*, Production Manager: *Arthur Alcott*, Assistant Director: *Billy Boyle*, Script: *Roland Pertwee*, Scenario Editor: *H. Ostrer*, Based on the novel by Lady Eleanor Smith, Director of Photography: *Stephen Dade*, Location Photography: *Cyril Knowles*, Editor: *Charles Knott*, Art Director: *John Bryan*, Musical Director: *Louis Levy*, Incidental Music: *Walford Hyden*, Choreography: *Cleo Nordi*, Costumes: *Elizabeth Haffenden*, Make-up: *W. Partleton*, Sound Supervisor: *B. C. Sewell*, Period Adviser: *Cyril Hartman*

Cast
Stewart Granger *Richard Darrell*, Jean Kent *Rosal*, Anne Crawford *Oriana*, Dennis Price *Francis*, Robert Helpmann *Wycroft* , Gerard Hinze *Don Carlos*, Enid Stamp Taylor *Bertha*, David Horne *Camperdene*, John Salew *Diego*, Arthur Goullet *Suiza*, Julian Somers *Manoel*, Peter Murray *Juan*, Gypsy Petulengro *Paco*, Sylvie St Clair *Marie*, Henry Morell *Cumbermere*, Victoria Campbell *Fanny*, Mabel Constanduros *Woman*, Josef Ramart *Jose*, Erin de Selfa *Singer in Cafe*, Philip Guard *Young Francis*, Peter Mullins *Young Richard*, Jacqueline Boyer *Young Oriana*

Nineteenth-century London. Richard Darrell, an impoverished aspiring writer, saves the life of Don Carlos, a wealthy Spanish diamond merchant. Richard tells the Spaniard the story of his life: The son of a doctor father and gypsy mother,

Richard spent much of his youth in the company of gypsies. He befriended Oriana, the daughter of the local squire, much to the chagrin of young Francis, his rival for Oriana's affections. When Oriana and Richard grew up, they decided to marry, but Oriana's father's debts necessitated a delay of one year, during which time Richard went to London to make his fortune. The year is now up, and Richard is still poor and unpublished. On hearing this, Don Carlos offers Richard a commission in Spain. Meanwhile, Oriana's father dies, leaving her penniless and at the mercy of the unscrupulous Francis, who wants to marry her. Richard leaves for Granada, promising to marry Oriana on his return, when Don Carlos will have arranged for his book to be published.

Francis despatches his sidekick, Wycroft, to Spain to arrange Richard's death. Wycroft employs a group of gypsies to ambush Richard. They leave him for dead, but he is found by Rosal, a gypsy dancer he met in Malaga, who takes him to her cave in the hills to recover. Richard has lost his memory, and Rosal convinces him that he loves her. Meanwhile, Francis persuades Oriana that Richard is dead and reluctantly she agrees to marry him. As soon as they are married, he treats her in an insulting and humiliating manner.

Richard begins to recover his memory. He goes to Granada to find Don Carlos's house, and learns about Oriana's marriage to Francis. Embittered, he writes Oriana an angry letter and returns to Rosal. Later, they are married in a gypsy ceremony. Oriana receives Richard's letter. Realising that he is alive after all, she leaves Francis and seeks out Don Carlos, who tells her that Richard is a wanted man in Spain. Oriana leaves for Granada to find Richard and clear his name. At Don Carlos's house, she meets Richard and learns of his marriage to Rosal. Francis and Wycroft have followed Oriana to Spain, and Francis tries to win Oriana back, but she refuses him. Richard returns to Rosal, who determines to prove his innocence.

Rosal tells Don Carlos the true perpetrators of Richard's ambush, and she and Oriana come face to face. Oriana persuades Rosal that she must clear Richard's name, even if it means losing him. Oriana confronts Francis and Wycroft, who determine to dispose of Rosal. They go to the tavern where she is to dance, followed by Oriana and Don Carlos. Richard sees Francis and Wycroft, and a fight breaks out. Francis shoots at Richard, but Rosal steps between them and is killed. Francis and Wycroft escape in Don Carlos's carriage, taking Oriana with them. Richard chases them on horseback. Wycroft is thrown from the carriage, which overturns. Richard pursues Francis into quicksands, where the latter is swallowed up. Richard and Oriana return to England.

The Magic Bow (1946)
Production Company: *Gainsborough*, Director: *Bernard Knowles*, Executive Producer: *Maurice Ostrer*, Producer: *R. J. Minney*, Production Supervisor: *Albert Fennell*, Production Manager: *Fred Gunn*, Assistant Director: *Douglas Peirce*, Script: *Roland Pertwee*, Based on the novel by Manuel Komroff, Additional Dialogue: *Norman Ginsbury*, Scenario Editor: *H. Ostrer*, Director of Photography: *Jack Cox*, Editor: *Alfred Roome*, Art Director: *Andrew Mazzei*, Set Design: *John*

Bryan, Special Effects: *Guidobaldi, A. Jullion*, Musical Director: *Louis Levy*, Music: *'Caprice No. 20', 'Violin Concerto No. 1', 'Campanella', 'Introduction and Variations' by Paganini; 'Violin Concerto Opus 61' by Beethoven; 'The Devil's Trill' by Tartini; 'La Ronde des Lutins' by Brazzini; 'Romance' by Phil Green, based on a theme by Paganini*, Incidental Music: *Henry Geehl*, Violin Solos Performed by: *Yehudi Menuhin*, accompanied by the *National Symphony Orchestra*, conducted by: *Basil Cameron*, Music Editor: *Bretton Byrd*, Costumes: *Elizabeth Haffenden*, Make-up: *W. Partleton*, Sound Supervisor: *B. C. Sewell*, Period Adviser: *Cyril Hartman*, Music Coach: *David McCallum*

Cast
Stewart Granger *Nicolo Paganini*, Phyllis Calvert *Jeanne de Vermond*, Jean Kent *Bianchi*, Dennis Price *Paul de la Rochelle*, Cecil Parker *Germi*, Marie Lohr *Countess de Vermond*, Henry Edwards *Count de Vermond*, Frank Cellier *Antonio*, Mary Jerrold *Teresa*, Betty Warren *Landlady*, Anthony Holles *Manager*, David Horne *Rizzi*, Robert Speaight *Cardinal*, Charles Victor *Peasant Driver*, Eliot Makeham *Giuseppe*, O. B. Clarence *Old Gentleman*, Felix Aylmer *Pasini*

Genoa, during Napoleon's advance on Italy. Impoverished and temperamental violinist Nicolo Paganini is employed by a beautiful young French aristocrat, Jeanne de Vermond, to play while her father escapes from jail. Paganini decides to go to Parma, where Signor Pasini is offering a Stradivarius to anyone who can play his difficult composition. On the road, he meets Germi, a lawyer who offers to become his manager. They find lodgings in Parma, and Paganini wins the Stradivarius. He is invited by Jeanne to play for her mother and her friends, but storms out when they fail to pay attention. He finds solace with Bianchi, a singer who has followed him from Genoa. When he loses all his money gambling, he pawns the Stradivarius. Jeanne redeems the violin and secretly returns it to Germi. At a public concert, Paganini's performance is interrupted by the arrival of French soldiers, led by Paul de la Rochelle, a suitor of Jeanne's who has spent some time in England. Paganini refuses to stop playing, and the French leave the concert hall. To Bianchi's chagrin, Paganini goes off with Jeanne after the concert. They pledge their love. But when Jeanne returns home, her mother announces that they are to return to Paris, where Jeanne will be married to Paul.

Jeanne and Paganini plan to run away and get married, until Jeanne's mother tells her that her marriage to Paul is by the Emperor's decree, and if she disobeys, her father will be punished. Jeanne and Paganini part, and the violinist embarks on a concert tour of Europe. Embittered by his experience with Jeanne, Paganini becomes a notorious womaniser. In Paris, he catches sight of Jeanne, who cuts him dead. Paganini sends a note to Jeanne inviting her to his concert that evening, whereupon Paul challenges him to a duel. Bianchi goes to see Jeanne, and they intervene, but not before Paganini is wounded in the hand. Paganini returns to Genoa to recover, but he has lost the will to play.

Bianchi visits Jeanne again and asks her to use her influence to help Paganini.

The violinist receives a command from the Vatican to play before the Pope. Jeanne, her mother and Paul attend the recital, where the Pope confers a knighthood on Paganini. Despite his fears of failure, Paganini plays for Jeanne, who now realises she can never marry Paul. She tells Paul her decision, then returns to the recital to enjoy Paganini's triumph.

So Long at the Fair (1950)
Production Company: *Gainsborough*, Directors: *Terence Fisher, Anthony Darnborough*, In Charge of Production: *Sydney Box*, Producer: *Betty E. Box*, Associate Producer: *Vivian Cox*, Production Controller: *Arthur Alcott*, Production Manager: *Billy Boyle*, Assistant Director: *Gerald O'Hara*, Script: *Hugh Mills, Anthony Thorne*, Based on the novel by Anthony Thorne, Director of Photography: *Reginald Wyer*, Camera Operator: *David Harcourt*, Editor: *Gordon Hales*, Supervising Art Director: *George Provis*, Art Director: *Cedric Dawe*, Special Effects: *Bill Warrington, Leslie Bowie*, Music/Musical Director: *Benjamin Frankel*, Costumes: *Elizabeth Haffenden*, Make-up: *George Blackler*, Sound Recordists: *S. Lambourne, Gordon McCallum*

Cast
Jean Simmons *Vicky Barton*, Dirk Bogarde *George Hathaway*, David Tomlinson *Johnny Barton*, Marcel Poncin *Narcisse Hervé*, Cathleen Nesbitt *Mme Hervé*, Honor Blackman *Rhoda O'Donovan*, Betty Warren *Mrs O'Donovan*, Eugene Deckers *Day Porter*, Zena Marshall *Nina*, Felix Aylmer *British Consul*, André Morell *Dr Hart*, Austin Trevor *Police Commissioner*, Natasha Sokolova *Charlotte*, Nelly Arno *Madame Verni*

Paris, 1889. Victoria Barton and her brother John arrive in Paris to visit the Exposition. Vicky is entranced by the city, but Johnny is more sceptical. After dining out they return to the hotel, where Vicky goes to bed, leaving Johnny to his nightcap. Johnny is approached by George Hathaway, a young English painter escorting his friends Mrs O'Donovan and her daughter Rhoda back to the hotel; Hathaway borrows money from him to pay for their cab. The next day, Vicky goes to collect Johnny from his room, only to find that both Johnny and the room itself have disappeared. The hotel concierge, Mme Hervé, and her brother Narcisse are unhelpful, insisting that Vicky booked in alone; the porter supports their story. Increasingly distraught, Vicky goes to see the British consul, who advises her to get evidence that Johnny was at the hotel. They go to the exhibition to look for a chambermaid who spoke to Vicky the evening of her arrival in Paris, and whose fiancé is flying a hot air balloon at the fair.

The balloon catches fire with the maid and her fiancé aboard, and both are killed. Vicky goes to the police, and the commissioner returns to the hotel with her to question Mme Hervé and Narcisse. They refuse to change their story, implying that Vicky is mad. Meanwhile, George Hathaway asks Mrs O'Donovan and Rhoda to deliver a note with the money he owes Johnny to the hotel. The desk clerk denies all knowledge of Johnny and room number nineteen. Next day,

Mme Hervé instructs Narcisse to accompany Vicky to the station where she can take the train for the ferry back to England. Vicky jumps off the train when Narcisse leaves. After opening the letter from George, delivered to her room by Rhoda, Vicky realises that he can support her story and she goes to his studio to ask his help.

George books a room at the hotel and smuggles Vicky in wearing masquerade costume. He discovers locked shutters to a room which does not appear to have an entrance in the hotel. Together, Vicky and George break into an adjoining room, and through the connecting doors into the sealed room, where they find evidence of Johnny's presence. Questioned by the commissioner, Mme Hervé confesses that Johnny became very ill during the night, and was taken away to a nearby convent. Vicky and George pick up an English doctor, Dr Hart, and go to the convent. There they discover that Johnny has contracted bubonic plague. Dr Hart tells Vicky that her brother is seriously ill, but has a chance of survival. Vicky and George leave the convent.

BIBLIOGRAPHY OF WORKS CITED

Articles and Chapters

Aspinall, Sue (1983), 'Sexuality in Costume Melodrama', in Aspinall, Sue, and Murphy, Robert (eds.), *BFI Dossier No. 18: Gainsborough Melodrama* (London: British Film Institute).

Berger, John (1991), 'Every Time We Say Goodbye', *Sight and Sound* vol. 1 no. 2 (June).

Bergfelder, Tim (1996), 'German Film Technicians in 30s Britain and the Emergence of the Production Designer', in Higson, Andrew (ed.), *Dissolving Views: Key Articles on British Cinema* (London: Cassell).

Bond, Ralph (1945), 'What Is the Future of British Films?', *Picture Post*, 6 January.

Christie, Ian (1978), 'The Scandal of *Peeping Tom*', in Christie, Ian (ed.), *Powell, Pressburger and Others*, (London: British Film Institute).

Cook, Pam (1983), 'Melodrama and the Women's Picture', in Aspinall and Murphy, *BFI Dossier No 18: Gainsborough Melodrama*.

Dawson, Graham, and West, Bob (1984), 'Our Finest Hour', in Hurd, Geoff (ed.), *National Fictions: World War Two in Film and Television* (London: BFI Publishing).

Donald, James (1992), 'How English Is It?', in Donald, James, *Sentimental Education: Schooling, Popular Culture and the Regulation of Liberty* (London: Verso).

Dyer, Richard (1994), 'Feeling English', *Sight and Sound* vol. 4 no. 3 (March).

Eckert, Charles (1990), 'The Carole Lombard in Macy's Window', in Gaines, Jane and Herzog, Charlotte (eds.), *Fabrications: Costume and the Female Body* (London and New York: Routledge).

Eco, Umberto (1995), 'Lumbar Thought', in *Faith in Fakes: Travels in Hyperreality* (London: Minerva).

Ellis, John (1975), 'Made in Ealing', *Screen* vol. 16 no. 1 (Spring).

Ellis, John (1978), 'Art, Culture and Quality: Terms for a Cinema in the Forties and Seventies', *Screen* vol. 19 no. 3 (Autumn). Reprinted in revised version in Higson, *Dissolving Views*.

Elsaesser, Thomas (1987), 'Tales of Sound and Fury', in Gledhill, Christine (ed.),

Home Is Where the Heart Is: Studies in Melodrama and the Women's Film (London: BFI Publishing).

Fletcher, Helen (1944), 'Review of *Madonna of the Seven Moons*', *Time and Tide*, 23 December.

Freud, Sigmund (1977a), 'Three Essays on the Theory of Sexuality (1905): I: The Sexual Aberrations', in *Pelican Freud Library Vol. 7* (Harmondsworth: Penguin Books).

Freud, Sigmund (1977b), 'Fetishism (1927)', in *Pelican Freud Library Vol. 7* (Harmondsworth: Penguin Books).

Freud, Sigmund (1979), 'A Child Is Being Beaten: A Contribution to the Study of the Origins of Sexual Perversions', in *Pelican Freud Library Vol. 10* (Harmondsworth: Penguin Books).

Freud, Sigmund (1990), 'The "Uncanny" (1919)', in *Pelican Freud Library Vol. 14* (Harmondsworth: Penguin Books).

Gaines, Jane (1990), 'Costume and Narrative: How Dress Tells the Woman's Story', in Gaines and Herzog, *Fabrications*.

Gott, Richard (1994), 'Stars in Our Eyes, Bars in Our Hearts', *Guardian*, 26 March.

Grigor, Murray (1982), 'From Scott-land to Disneyland', in McArthur, Colin (ed.), *Scotch Reels: Scotland in Cinema and Television* (London: BFI Publishing).

Harper, Sue (1983), 'Art Direction and Costume Design', in Aspinall and Murphy, *BFI Dossier No. 18: Gainsborough Melodrama*. Reprinted in revised version in Gledhill, *Home Is Where the Heart Is*.

Harper, Sue (1988), 'The Representation of Women in British Feature Films, 1939–1945', in Taylor, Philip (ed.), *Britain and the Cinema in the Second World War* (Basingstoke and London: Macmillan).

Higson, Andrew (1984), 'Addressing the Nation', in Hurd, *National Fictions*.

Higson, Andrew (1993a), 'Re-presenting the National Past: Nostalgia and Pastiche in the Heritage Film', in Friedman, Lester (ed.), *British Cinema and Thatcherism: Fires Were Started* (London: UCL Press).

Higson, Andrew (1993b), 'Between Film Europe and Hollywood: German Emigrés and the British Film Industry, 1927–1939', in Dunkhase, Gerke (ed.), *London Calling* (Munich: Edition Text + Kritik). In German.

Hollander, Anne (1974), 'The "Gatsby Look" and Other Costume Movie Blunders', *New York* 7 No. 21, 27 May.

Johnston, Claire (1975), 'Femininity and the Masquerade: *Anne of the Indies*', in Johnston, Claire and Willemen, Paul (eds.), *Jacques Tourneur*, (Edinburgh: Edinburgh Film Festival).

Light, Alison (1988), '"Young Bess": Historical Novels and Growing Up', *Feminist Review* 33 (Autumn).

Lochhead, Liz (1995), 'The Shadow', *Sight and Sound* vol. 5 no. 6 (June).

McArthur, Colin (1984), 'National Identities', in Hurd, *National Fictions*.

Mace, Nigel (1988), 'British Historical Epics in the Second World War', in Taylor, *Britain and the Cinema in the Second World War*.

Maeder, Edward (1987), 'The Celluloid Image: Historical Dress in Film', in

Maeder, Edward (ed.), *Hollywood and History: Costume Design in Film* (Los Angeles and London: Los Angeles County Museum of Art/Thames and Hudson).

Modleski, Tania (1991), 'A Father Is Being Beaten: Male Feminism and the War Film', in Modleski, Tania, *Feminism Without Women: Culture and Criticism in a 'Postfeminist' Age* (London and New York: Routledge).

Mulvey, Laura (1987), 'Notes on Sirk and Melodrama', in Gledhill, *Home Is Where the Heart Is.*

Mulvey, Laura (1989a), 'Visual Pleasure and Narrative Cinema', in Mulvey, *Visual and Other Pleasures* (Basingstoke and London: Macmillan).

Mulvey, Laura (1989b), 'Afterthoughts on "Visual Pleasure and Narrative Cinema" inspired by King Vidor's *Duel in the Sun* (1946)', in Mulvey, *Visual and Other Pleasures.*

Murphy, Robert (1983), 'A Brief Studio History', in Aspinall and Murphy, *BFI Dossier No. 18: Gainsborough Melodrama.*

Murphy, Robert (1984), 'British Film Production 1939–45', in Hurd, *National Fictions.*

Murphy, Robert (1988), 'The British Film Industry: Audiences and Producers', in Taylor, *Britain and the Cinema in the Second World War.*

Nowell-Smith, Geoffrey (1987), 'Minnelli and Melodrama', in Gledhill, *Home Is Where the Heart Is.*

Petley, Julian (1986), 'The Lost Continent', in Barr, Charles (ed.), *All Our Yesterdays: Ninety Years of British Cinema* (London: British Film Institute).

Phillips, Pearson (1963), 'The New Look', in Sissons, Michael and French, Philip (eds.), *Age of Austerity: 1945–1951* (Oxford: Oxford University Press).

Richards, Jeffrey, 'National Identity in British Wartime Films', in Taylor, *Britain and the Cinema in the Second World War.*

Seaton, Ray and Martin, Roy (1982a), 'Gainsborough', *Films and Filming* (May).

Seaton, Ray and Martin, Roy (1982b), 'Gainsborough in the 40s', *Films and Filming* (June).

Studlar, Gaylyn (1990), 'Masochism, Masquerade and the Erotic Metamorphoses of Marlene Dietrich', in Gaines and Herzog, *Fabrications.*

Turim, Maureen (1990), 'Designing Women: The Emergence of the New Sweetheart Line', in Gaines and Herzog, *Fabrications.*

Books

Aspinall, Sue and Murphy, Robert (1983) (eds.), *BFI Dossier No 18: Gainsborough Melodrama* (London: British Film Institute).

Barr, Charles (1977), *Ealing Studios* (London: Cameron and Tayleur in association with David and Charles).

Barr, Charles (1986) (ed.), *All Our Yesterdays: Ninety Years of British Cinema* (London: BFI Publishing).

Christie, Ian (1978), *Powell, Pressburger and Others* (London: British Film Institute).

Christie, Ian (1985), *Arrows of Desire* (London: Waterstone).

Corner, John and Harvey, Sylvia (1991) (eds.), *Enterprise and Heritage: Cross-currents of National Culture* (London and New York: Routledge).

Custen, George F. (1992), *Bio/Pics: How Hollywood Constructed Public History* (New Brunswick, NJ: Rutgers University Press).

DelGaudio, Sybil (1993), *Dressing the Part: Sternberg, Dietrich and Costume* (London and Toronto: Associated University Presses).

Donald, James (1992), *Sentimental Education: Schooling, Popular Culture and the Regulation of Liberty* (London: Verso).

Durgnat, Raymond (1970), *A Mirror for England* (London: Faber).

Foucault, Michel (1974), *The Archaeology of Knowledge* (London: Tavistock).

Gaines, Jane and Herzog, Charlotte (1990) (eds.), *Fabrications: Costume and the Female Body* (London and New York: Routledge).

Garber, Marjorie (1992), *Vested Interests: Cross-dressing and Cultural Anxiety* (London and New York: Routledge).

Gledhill, Christine (1987) (ed.), *Home Is Where the Heart Is: Studies in Melodrama and the Women's Film* (London: BFI Publishing).

Harper, Sue (1994), *Picturing the Past: The Rise and Fall of the British Costume Film* (London: BFI Publishing).

Higson, Andrew (1995), *Waving the Flag: Constructing a National Cinema in Britain* (Oxford: Clarendon Press).

Higson, Andrew (1996) (ed.), *Dissolving Views: Key Articles on British Cinema* (London: Cassell).

Hurd, Geoff (1984) (ed.), *National Fictions: World War Two in British Film and Television* (London: BFI Publishing).

Kuhn, Annette (1985), *The Power of the Image: Essays on Representation and Sexuality* (London, Boston, Melbourne and Henley: Routledge and Kegan Paul).

Kulik, Karol (1975), *Alexander Korda: The Man Who Could Work Miracles* (London: W. H. Allen).

Landy, Marcia (1991), *British Genres: Cinema and Society, 1930–1960* (Princeton, NJ: Princeton University Press).

Lant, Antonia (1991), *Blackout: Reinventing Women for Wartime British Cinema* (Princeton, NJ: Princeton University Press).

Leese, Elizabeth (1991), *Costume Design in the Movies: An Illustrated Guide to the Work of 157 Great Designers* (New York: Dover Publications).

Light, Alison (1991), *Forever England: Femininity, Literature and Conservatism Between the Wars* (London and New York: Routledge).

McArthur, Colin (1982) (ed.), *Scotch Reels: Scotland in Cinema and Television* (London: BFI Publishing).

Maeder, Edward (1987) (ed.), *Hollywood and History: Costume Design in Film* (Los Angeles and London: Los Angeles County Museum of Art/Thames and Hudson).

Modleski, Tania (1988), *The Women Who Knew Too Much: Hitchcock and Feminist Theory* (London and New York: Methuen).

Tania Modleski (1991), *Feminism Without Women: Culture and Criticism in a 'Post-Feminist' Age* (London and New York: Routledge).

125

Murphy, Robert (1992), *Realism and Tinsel: Cinema and Society in Britain 1939–1949* (London and New York: Routledge).

Pevsner, Nikolaus (1956), *The Englishness of English Art* (Harmondsworth: Penguin Books).

Pirie, David (1973), *A Heritage of Horror* (London: Gordon Fraser).

Richards, Jeffrey and Sheridan, Dorothy (1987) (eds.), *Mass-Observation at the Movies* (London and New York: Routledge and Kegan Paul).

Salmi, Markku (1982) (ed.), *National Film Archive Catalogue of Stills, Posters and Designs* (London: British Film Institute).

Sorlin, Pierre (1980), *The Film in History: Restaging the Past* (Oxford: Blackwell).

Stallybrass, Peter and White, Allon (1986), *The Politics and Poetics of Transgression* (London: Methuen).

Surowiec, Catherine A. (1996), *Cinema Design* (London: British Film Institute).

Taylor, Philip M. (1988) (ed.), *Britain and the Cinema in the Second World War* (Basingstoke: Macmillan).

Williams, Linda (1990), *Hard Core: Power, Pleasure and the 'Frenzy of the Visible'* (London: Pandora).

Wilson, Elizabeth (1985), *Adorned in Dreams: Fashion and Modernity* (London: Virago).

FILMS CITED

(Titles, countries and dates taken from Salmi, 1982)

Adventures of Tartu, The	UK	1943	(MGM British)
Anne of the Indies	USA	1951	(20th Century Fox)
Bad Lord Byron, The	UK	1949	(Triton)
Bank Holiday	UK	1938	(Gainsborough)
Blanche Fury	UK	1947	(Cineguild)
Builders	UK	1942	(Crown Film Unit)
Canterbury Tale, A	UK	1944	(Archers)
Caravan	UK	1946	(Gainsborough)
Catherine the Great	UK	1934	(London Films)
Chariots of Fire	UK/USA	1981	(Enigma)
Christopher Columbus	UK	1949	(Gainsborough)
Comin' Thro' the Rye	UK	1923	(Hepworth Picture Plays)
Daughters of the Dust	USA	1991	(American Playhouse)
Demi-Paradise, The	UK	1943	(Anatole de Grunwald)
Duel in the Sun	USA	1946	(Selznick International)
Edward II	UK	1991	(Working Title)
Gentle Sex, The	UK	1943	(Concanen)
Hamlet	UK	1948	(Two Cities)
Henry V	UK	1944	(Two Cities)
In Which We Serve	UK	1942	(Two Cities)
Jassy	UK	1947	(Gainsborough)
Johnny Frenchman	UK	1945	(Ealing)
June Bride	USA	1948	(Warner Bros)

Lady Vanishes, The	UK	1939	(Gainsborough)
Lodger, The	UK/Germany	1926	(Gainsborough)
Madonna of the Seven Moons	UK	1944	(Gainsborough)
Magic Bow, The	UK	1946	(Gainsborough)
Man in Grey, The	UK	1943	(Gainsborough)
Maytime in Mayfair	UK	1949	(Imperadio)
Millions Like Us	UK	1943	(Gainsborough)
Mrs Miniver	USA	1942	(Loew's Incorporated)
Orlando	UK/Russia/ France/Italy/ Netherlands	1993	(Adventure Films)
Passport to Pimlico	UK	1949	(Ealing)
Peeping Tom	UK	1959	(Michael Powell Theatre)
Perfect Strangers	UK	1945	(MGM British)
Piano, The	Australia/ France	1993	(Jan Chapman)
Pleasure Garden, The	UK/Germany	1925	(Gainsborough)
Rear Window	USA	1954	(Patron, Inc)
Rebecca	USA	1940	(David Selznick)
Rob Roy	USA	1995	(Talisman)
Scarlet Empress, The	USA	1934	(Paramount)
So Long at the Fair	UK	1950	(Gainsborough)
Sylvia Scarlett	USA	1935	(RKO)
This Happy Breed	UK	1944	(Two Cities)
Tudor Rose	UK	1936	(Gainsborough)
Vertigo	USA	1958	(Paramount)
Waterloo Road	UK	1944	(Gainsborough)
Way Ahead, The	UK	1944	(Two Cities)
Wicked Lady, The	UK	1945	(Gainsborough)
Wings of the Morning	UK	1936	(New World Pictures)

ELIZABETH HAFFENDEN
COSTUME DESIGNER

Biofilmography
(Information compiled from Salmi, 1982, Aspinall and Murphy, 1983, Leese, 1991, and publicity material held by the British Film Institute. Additional information provided by Catherine Surowiec. Maeder, 1987, p. 123, incorrectly lists Haffenden's country of origin as USA.)

Elizabeth Haffenden had a long and illustrious career in theatre and cinema, spanning more than forty years. She was born in Croydon, England, in 1906 and died in London in 1976. She attended Croydon School of Art and the Royal College of Art, becoming a commercial artist before moving into theatre costume design during the 30s, in association with production designer Laurence Irving. Her first job in the film industry was with Sound City, subsequently Shepperton Studios, in 1933 (Leese, 1991). Together with René Hubert she contributed to several Alexander Korda productions, including *The Thief of Bagdad* (UK, 1940).

Haffenden continued to work in theatre until the 1950s, but joined Gaumont-British in 1939, and from 1942 to 1949 was in charge of the Gainsborough costume department at Shepherd's Bush. She is credited by the studio with having predicted in 1944 the post-war swing to glamorous, New Look-style fashions, and with having a particular interest in the use of colour in photography. In the 50s, after the demise of Gainsborough, she was resident costume designer at MGM British, Elstree/Borehamwood, and from the late 50s worked freelance.

As the following filmography indicates, Haffenden specialised in designs for historical drama, a genre in which film studies has shown little interest until recently. From 1959, she consistently worked in association with her close friend, Technicolor consultant Joan Bridge, whom she first met at Gainsborough in 1946. They won Academy Awards for *Ben-Hur* (USA, 1959) and *A Man For All Seasons* (UK, 1966), and BAFTA award nominations for *The Amorous Adventures of Moll Flanders* (UK, 1965) and *Half a Sixpence* (UK/USA, 1967). They also received a BAFTA award for *A Man For All Seasons*.

Films
1933 *Colonel Blood* (UK, W. P. Lipscomb)
A seventeenth-century historical drama, produced by Sound City, this was
Haffenden's first job in the film industry. Laurence Irving and John Bryan were
the art directors.
1936 *Wedding Group* (UK, Alex Bryce, Campbell Gullan)
Produced by Fox British Pictures, this is a period romantic drama about jealousy
and betrayal set in Scotland and the Crimea. It featured Fay Compton as
Florence Nightingale and was praised by the *Monthly Film Bulletin* (*MFB*) for its
authenticity, despite occasional lapses into caricature.
1939 *Ten Days in Paris* (UK, Tim Whelan)
A comedy mystery set in Paris, starring Rex Harrison as an Englishman who
becomes entangled in a web of intrigue involving a gang of spies and a drama of
mistaken identities.
The Spy in Black (UK, Michael Powell)
This U-boat espionage drama, set in the Orkneys during the First World War,
was admired by the *MFB* for its suspense, realism and convincing performances.
Conrad Veidt was singled out for his brilliant portrayal of the sinister yet tragic
hero.
1942 *The Young Mr Pitt* [with Cecil Beaton] (UK, Carol Reed)
Edward Black was the producer of this ambitious political drama, scripted by
Launder and Gilliat and, in the opinion of the *MFB*, demonstrating only minor
faults of historical inaccuracy.
1943 *The Man in Grey* (UK, Leslie Arliss)
The first of the 40s Gainsborough costume cycle, set in contemporary wartime
Britain with flashbacks to the 18th century, and featuring members of the
studio's star stable: Phyllis Calvert, Stewart Granger, Margaret Lockwood and a
glowering James Mason.
Dear Octopus (UK, Harold French)
Produced by Edward Black and scripted by R. J. Minney, this Gainsborough
production about a family reunion starred Margaret Lockwood and Michael
Wilding, with Arthur Crabtree as cinematographer and John Bryan as art
director. The *MFB* praised Celia Johnson's performance as the long-lost
daughter with a past.
1944 *Fanny by Gaslight* (UK, Anthony Asquith)
Gainsborough period melodrama in the 'gaslight' mode, scripted by Doreen
Montgomery and Aimee Stuart from the Michael Sadleir novel and produced by
Edward Black. The *MFB* admired the meticulous period authenticity.
Love Story (UK, Leslie Arliss)
Gainsborough romantic wartime melodrama set in Cornwall and featuring
Margaret Lockwood, Stewart Granger and Patricia Roc in a love triangle.
Madonna of the Seven Moons (UK, Arthur Crabtree)
Set in Italy in the late 30s, this Gainsborough melodrama deals with the
'schizophrenia' of its heroine, played by Phyllis Calvert, who is torn between
home and respectability and adulterous passion.

A Place of One's Own (UK, Bernard Knowles)
Based on the novel by Osbert Sitwell, this Gothic drama, produced by Gainsborough, has an uncanny theme in which a house has a mysterious influence on its inhabitants.
Give Us the Moon (UK, Val Guest)
Gainsborough comedy, adapted from a novel by Caryl Brahms and S. J. Simon, about a society called The Elephants whose guiding principle is complete disregard for work. It starred Margaret Lockwood and Vic Oliver, with a young Jean Simmons playing an eleven-year-old brat.
Two Thousand Women (UK, Frank Launder)
Set in a women's internment camp in France during the Second World War, this is the story of the inmates' attempts to smuggle out some British airmen who inadvertently parachute into the camp one night. Produced by Gainsborough and scripted by Launder and Gilliat, it featured excellent performances from Phyllis Calvert, Flora Robson and a sultry Jean Kent.
1945 *The Wicked Lady* (UK, Leslie Arliss)
Flamboyantly sexual Gainsborough costume drama, set in Restoration England and following the escapades of the tomboy Lady Skelton, played by Margaret Lockwood. Terence Fisher worked as editor and John Bryan was art director.
I'll Be Your Sweetheart (UK, Val Guest)
A Gainsborough musical, set in 1900, about the legal battles to institute copyright protection for songwriters and publishers. The *MFB* praised Margaret Lockwood's lively performance.
1946 *Caravan* (UK, Arthur Crabtree)
Gainsborough period romance set in nineteenth-century England and Spain, starring Stewart Granger as an impoverished writer who falls in love with a Spanish gypsy (Jean Kent) while suffering from amnesia.
Bedelia (UK, Lance Comfort)
Scripted by Vera Caspary, who wrote the novel on which Otto Preminger's *Laura* (USA, 1944) was based, this *noir*-influenced film starred Margaret Lockwood as the eponymous husband-killer.
The Magic Bow (UK, Bernard Knowles)
Gainsborough historical romance, set in Italy during the Napoleonic wars, and (very) loosely based on the life of temperamental violinist Paganini, played by Stewart Granger.
1947 *The Man Within* (UK, Bernard Knowles)
Based on the novel by Graham Greene, this period smuggling drama featured a homoerotic sub-text and was shot in flamboyantly garish Technicolor.
Jassy (UK, Bernard Knowles)
This lurid Gainsborough period drama set in 1830 tells the rags to riches story of a gypsy woman, played by Margaret Lockwood. Contemporary critics noted the propensity for torture, flogging and bloodshed. The costumes made the most of the stunning Technicolor cinematography by Geoffrey Unsworth.
Uncle Silas (UK, Charles Frank)
An atmospheric period drama starring Jean Simmons as a young heiress who

goes to live with her uncle after her father's death, only to find that he is after her money. The *MFB* judged it too melodramatic.

1948 *Call of the Blood* (UK, John Clements)
Period drama of adultery, murder and suicide set in Sicily at the turn of the century, featuring a male protagonist of mixed British and Italian origin.
The First Gentleman (UK, Alberto Cavalcanti)
Produced by Columbia British, this historical drama set in the 18th century tells the tragic story of Princess Charlotte, daughter of the Prince Regent. The *MFB* praised its faithful historical reconstruction.

1949 *The Bad Lord Byron* (UK, David MacDonald)
Biography loosely based on the life of the notorious nineteenth-century poet and his involvement in various European causes and scandalous love affairs. Dennis Price played Byron with suitable patrician aplomb.
Christopher Columbus [with Joan Ellacott] (UK, David MacDonald)
Gainsborough's historical extravaganza, shot in Technicolor by Stephen Dade and following the exploits of the famous explorer, was considered ponderous by contemporary critics.
The Spider and the Fly (UK, Robert Hamer)
Set in Paris in 1913, this caper film, revolving around a battle of wills between a Raffles-style thief and a dour police chief, did not impress the *MFB*.

1950 *So Long at the Fair* (UK, Anthony Darnborough, Terence Fisher)
Beautifully photographed in black and white by Reginald Wyer, this decorative Gainsborough costume drama, based on the novel by Anthony Thorne and set in Paris in 1889, has a dark and pessimistic theme of cultural contamination. Apparently it was much admired by Alfred Hitchcock.
Portrait of Clare (UK, Lance Comfort)
A film about a woman's three marriages, based on the novel by Francis Brett Young.

1951 *The Late Edwina Black* (UK, Maurice Elvey)
Based on a successful stage production and dealing with the mysterious death of a village school teacher's domineering wife, this film was described by the *MFB* as an unpretentious Victorian thriller in the 'gaslight' mode.

1953 *The Story of Gilbert and Sullivan* [with Hein Heckroth] (UK, Sidney Gilliat)
Scripted by Launder and Gilliat for London Films, with Hein Heckroth as production designer and featuring Gilbert and Sullivan's music, this film nevertheless failed to impress the *MFB*.
Laughing Anne (UK, Herbert Wilcox)
Period drama based on a Joseph Conrad story about a stormy love affair between a sea captain and a French saloon singer, played by Margaret Lockwood.

1954 *Beau Brummell* (UK, Curtis Bernhardt)
Alfred Junge was the art director on this fanciful version of the Regency dandy's life and loves, featuring Stewart Granger and Elizabeth Taylor.
Invitation to the Dance [with Rolf Gerard] (UK, Gene Kelly)
A three-episode ballet film designed by Alfred Junge, without dialogue

and including animated sequences by Fred Quimby and Hanna and Barbera.

1955 *The Dark Avenger* (UK, Henry Levin)
Set during the 100 Years' War, this film followed the adventures of the Black Prince, played by Errol Flynn.

The Adventures of Quentin Durward (UK, Richard Thorpe)
Period romance based on the novel by Walter Scott and designed by Alfred Junge, with Robert Taylor as the fifteenth-century Scottish knight.

Footsteps in the Fog [with Beatrice Dawson] (UK, Arthur Lubin)
'Gaslight' drama set in Edwardian London, starring Jean Simmons as the housemaid who blackmails her murderous employer, Stewart Granger.

1956 *Bhowani Junction* (USA, George Cukor)
Story of an Anglo-Indian woman, played by Ava Gardner, torn between her attraction for an English soldier and the love of a young Sikh.

Moby Dick (USA, John Huston)
Scripted by Ray Bradbury and Huston, this version of Melville's novel focused on the obsessive quest of Captain Ahab, played by Gregory Peck, to kill the Great White Whale.

The Barretts of Wimpole Street (UK, Sidney A. Franklin)
An uninspired remake of Franklin's 1934 version of the love affair between Elizabeth Barrett and Robert Browning, with art direction by Alfred Junge.

The Little Hut (USA, Mark Robson)
Based on a play by André Roussin, this film, set on a desert island, featured Ava Gardner as Lady Susan Ashlow, neglected by her husband (Stewart Granger) and looking for romance with David Niven. According to the *MFB*, it was singularly lacking in wit and style.

1957 *The Shiralee* (UK, Leslie Norman)
Ealing's adaptation of the novel by D'Arcy Nyland had Peter Finch as the Australian husband who takes to the road with his young daughter.

Heaven Knows, Mr Allison (USA/UK, John Huston)
World War Two drama with Deborah Kerr as a nun and Robert Mitchum as a marine, an unlikely couple thrown together on a remote island threatened by Japanese invasion.

Davy (UK, Michael Relph)
Ealing backstage comedy with Harry Secombe as Davy, a member of a family variety act who has aspirations to become an opera singer.

I Accuse! (UK/USA, Jose Ferrer)
Scripted by Gore Vidal, this reconstruction of the Dreyfus case features Jose Ferrer as the Jew unjustly accused of treason in 1890s France.

1959 *Ben-Hur* [with Joan Bridge] (USA, William Wyler)
Blockbuster CinemaScope biblical epic starring Charlton Heston, for which Haffenden and Bridge's richly coloured and evocative costumes received an Academy Award.

1960 *The Sundowners* [with Joan Bridge] (UK/Australia, Fred Zinnemann)
Deborah Kerr and Robert Mitchum teamed up again for this story of a nomadic sheep drover and his family, set in 1920s Australia.

1961 *Hawaii* [with Joan Bridge] (USA, Fred Zinnemann)
Unrealised project.

1962 *Village of Daughters* (UK, George Pollock)
Comedy starring Eric Sykes as an English travelling salesman stranded in an Italian village full of beautiful women.

I Thank a Fool (UK, Robert Stevens)
A mystery with 'gaslight' overtones in which a doctor convicted of a mercy killing, played by Susan Hayward, becomes involved with a man and his invalid wife.

Kill or Cure [with Joan Bridge] (UK, George Pollock)
Comedy set in a health resort, in which Terry-Thomas and Eric Sykes set out to discover the murderer of a wealthy widow.

1964 *Behold a Pale Horse* [with Joan Bridge] (USA, Fred Zinnemann)
This drama, based on a novel by Emeric Pressburger, about the conflict between two old enemies of the Spanish Civil War (Gregory Peck and Anthony Quinn), was too 'international' for the *MFB*.

1965 *The Amorous Adventures of Moll Flanders* [with Joan Bridge] (UK, Terence Young)
Gainsborough veteran Alex Vetchinsky was the location art director on this lavish and colourful CinemaScope version of Defoe's novel, starring Kim Novak as Moll.

The Liquidator [with Joan Bridge] (UK, Jack Cardiff)
James Bond-style spy film featuring Rod Taylor as the reluctant secret agent who prefers bedroom capers to violence.

1966 *A Man For All Seasons* [with Joan Bridge] (UK, Fred Zinnemann)
Adapted from Robert Bolt's play about the trials and tribulations of Sir Thomas More, this film was praised by the *MFB* for its excellent production values. Haffenden and Bridge's costumes received Academy and BAFTA awards.

Drop Dead Darling [with Joan Bridge, Pierre Balmain] (UK, Ken Hughes)
A black comedy in which a gigolo, played by Tony Curtis, becomes rich by marrying and murdering wealthy women, until he meets his match in Rosanna Schiaffino.

1967 *Half a Sixpence* [with Joan Bridge] (UK/USA, George Sidney)
Big-budget musical based on the novel *Kipps* by H. G. Wells, starring Tommy Steele as the ordinary man who comes into a fortune and then loses it again.

1968 *Chitty Chitty Bang Bang* [with Joan Bridge] (UK, Ken Hughes)
Ken Adam was the production designer on this musical fantasy, based on short stories by Ian Fleming, about a nineteenth-century inventor, played by Dick Van Dyke.

The Prime of Miss Jean Brodie [with Joan Bridge] (UK, Ronald Neame)
Jay Presson Allen scripted this adaptation of her play based on Muriel Spark's novel, set in the 30s and starring Maggie Smith as the Scottish school teacher who allows her personal interests to override her duty.

1969 *Man's Fate* [with Joan Bridge] (USA, Fred Zinnemann)

Unrealised project. Scripted by Graham Greene from the book by André Malraux, this account of the crushing of the Communist insurrection in Shanghai in 1927 was abandoned by MGM.

1971 *Fiddler on the Roof* [with Joan Bridge] (USA, Norman Jewison)
Adaptation of the stage musical about a Jewish community in Czarist Russia, starring Topol, which the *MFB* compared unfavourably with the original.

1972 *Pope Joan* [with Joan Bridge] (UK, Michael Anderson)
Set in ninth-century Germany, a sombre account of the life of the legendary female pope, played by Liv Ullmann.

1973 *The Day of the Jackal* [with Joan Bridge, Rosine Delamare] (UK/France, Fred Zinnemann)
Thriller set in 1963 based on the novel by Frederick Forsythe about an assassination attempt on General de Gaulle, starring Edward Fox as the Jackal.

The Homecoming [with Joan Bridge] (USA/UK, Peter Hall)
Scripted by Harold Pinter from his own play about a family reunion and starring Cyril Cusack, Ian Holm and Vivien Merchant, this production was praised by the *MFB* as a successful film adaptation of the stage version.

Luther (USA/UK/Canada, Guy Green)
Based on John Osborne's play, which owed much to Brecht, this pedestrian account of the life of the sixteenth-century monk who became a major theological scholar starred Stacy Keach as Martin Luther.

1975 *Great Expectations* [with Joan Bridge] (UK, Joseph Hardy)
Made for American television, this adaptation of Dickens's novel, featuring a star-studded British cast, had a limited theatrical release outside the USA. The *MFB* preferred the 1946 David Lean version.

Conduct Unbecoming [with Joan Bridge] (UK, Michael Anderson)
In nineteenth-century India a young lieutenant, played by Michael York, is unjustly accused of assaulting an officer's widow and is put on trial before his fellow officers in the Indian Light Cavalry, with unexpected results.

1977 *Julia* [with Joan Bridge] (USA, Fred Zinnemann)
Haffenden started pre-production work with Joan Bridge on the costumes for this film, but died before production began. The costume design is credited to Anthea Sylbert, Joan Bridge and Annalisa Nasalli-Rocca.

NAME AND TITLE INDEX